# SUN YAT SEN
## AND THE
# CHINESE REPUBLIC

DR. SUN YAT SEN
Founder of the Chinese Republic.

# SUN YAT SEN
### AND THE
# CHINESE REPUBLIC

BY

## PAUL LINEBARGER

ILLUSTRATED WITH
PHOTOGRAPHS

AMS PRESS
NEW YORK

Reprinted from the edition of 1925, New York
First AMS EDITION published 1969
Manufactured in the United States of America


Library of Congress Catalogue Card Number: 70-96469


AMS PRESS, INC.
NEW YORK, N. Y. 10003

DEDICATED

TO

THE CHINESE NATIONALISTS

AND TO

THEIR DARE-TO-DIES

WHOSE GRAVES IN EVERY PROVINCE
OF CHINA, BEAR WITNESS TO THE
PEOPLE'S FAITH IN SUN YAT SEN

# FOREWORD

During the years 1901 to 1907, while the author was a circuit judge in the Philippines, he had in his service a very excellent Cantonese cook named Ah Po, whose attendance, during the sea voyages from court to court, was indeed appreciated, especially during the trying period of cholera epidemics, when the preparation of the food was a vital matter. This sentiment of appreciation developed into real gratitude when, on the occasion of a certain ship adventure, Ah Po saved the author's life.

Encouraged by this gratitude, Ah Po eventually confided that he was one of Sun Yat Sen's Dare-to-Dies and that he wanted a substantial loan and leave of absence to return to China. These requests being granted, faithful Ah Po went his way, and only after long weeks overdue did he return, more dead than alive. The Imperialists had caught him, put him on the torture rack, and finally thrown him out for dead. This brutality, together with Ah Po's direct information of Sun Yat Sen's program to establish a republic in China, made the author a partisan of Sun Yat Sen. If this torture-racked and body-broken untutored cook still had the courage to stand out for the ideals of his great leader, was it not the democratic duty of an American, in enjoyment of great privileges, to sympathize at all events, in some helpful way, with this liberty-loving effort of the Dare-to-Dies? So the author's heart warmed to Sun Yat Sen's movement, although, because of his judicial position, he held aloof from any direct participation. After his resignation as judge, however, the author became somewhat active in Dr. Sun's support, and, in 1913, he wrote a book, "Our Chinese Chances," which, in 1914, was circulated rather widely by Dr. Sun's party (the Kuo Ming Tong), with the purpose of defeating a loan sought by Yuan Shih Kai. In 1917, the author became the editor-in-chief of a monthly magazine, "The Chinese Nationalist." He also performed other propaganda work for the Kuo Ming Tong, supplementing this press work by the practice of his profession as a lawyer in their behalf, not only in China but in America and other jurisdictions as well.

For years the author had lamented frequently the lack of biographical information concerning

the great Reformer, for so insurmountable was
Sun's modesty that he had given out no detailed
information concerning himself, and particularly
of his early life. After much persuasion, in the
summer of 1919, Dr. Sun consented to give to the
author the time necessary to prepare the story
of his life, and, indeed, did devote many days
(with the author) to the assembling of such material. But, alas! the modesty of the Chinese
leader would always intervene at a crucial period;
and because of his absolute silence upon dramatic
situations, in which Dr. Sun was the central hero,
it has been necessary to supplement the information given by the Chinese leader by gleanings
from many sources, particularly from among the
few survivors of the oldest members of his following. To these is owing much of the matter
which may, by some, be termed eulogistic. Because of the various sources from which the
subject-matter is drawn, it has been found difficult to organize the narration so that extraneous
material, repetition, and hero-worship should not
affect the biographical data. Another difficulty
was that the biographical data could not be com-
posed upon any Occidental pattern, for, among
the Chinese, biographies are unknown as demanded by the man of the West. Still another
difficulty was the coördinating of biographical

data with information concerning China, for the average Occidental reader is not well informed concerning Chinese social or political life, and hence would not understand Sun's life without having a collateral story of China told at the same time. Certain phases of Sun's political activity would entail much more of an explanation than the limits of a popular volume would allow. It has been found necessary to cut the original manuscript down to less than half of its original composition. Reducing the size of the manuscript has exacted six complete revisions and rewritings, and the author hopes that at length he has given the Occidental at least something of an understandable picture of the Chinese Reformer in the following episodic chapters.

The author has not involved this work with much reference to the terrible struggles now going on in China between Sun Yat Sen and the Chinese masses on the one hand, as against Peking militarism, supported by certain banking and commercial interests of Japan and of certain Christian lands, on the other. This is an argumentative field beyond the purview of the volume. The author, however, voices the hope that the present *tuchun* war in China will awaken, eventually, American democracy to the great need of protecting its own institutions by supporting the

Chinese Republic as founded through the moral force of Sun Yat Sen.

The author has to thank Mrs. Sun for many of the illustrations, some of which are the only ones of their kind. He has, likewise, to thank a member of the Sun family for the chapter on "Domestic Relations," a delicate subject with which he did not dare deal without confidential assistance.

The author takes this opportunity to express his appreciation of the many days of generous hospitality which it has been his honor to enjoy in the happy and hospitable, though temporary, domicile of the Founder of the Chinese Republic.

PAUL LINEBARGER.

62 Kiangse Road,
Shanghai, China.

# CONTENTS

# CONTENTS

# CONTENTS

# ILLUSTRATIONS

xvii

# ILLUSTRATIONS

# FIRST PERIOD

### 1866 to 1879
### EARLY CHINESE LIFE

# SUN YAT SEN AND THE CHINESE REPUBLIC

## I

### THE TOWN OF BLUE VALLEY

CHOY HUNG, the Town of Blue Valley, with the purple mountain of the Plowshare for its background; the hamlet in the Vale of Blue! Just another of the tens of thousands of Chinese Sleepy Hollows, a few flecks and broken lines in white and gray in the tropical green of a valley whose mountains are blue.

It was in our Christian year 1866 that a certain "boy mouth" came as an addition to this little wayside Town of Blue Valley. It does not matter about the day of the lunar month, for Chinese do not generally hold age enumeration with Occidental exactness, their universal birthday being the Chinese New Year, when every one counts another communal year of his life. So that, in the Chinese New Year that fell in 1867, the little one —afterward known as Sun Yat Sen—according to Chinese calculations, was already two years old;

3

although in fact, from our Christian calculation, he was younger than this, for a Chinese child who is born even the day before the Chinese New Year is two years of age the day after.[1]

I shall set to rest here the wide-spread and erroneous report of Sun Yat Sen's [2] having been born in Honolulu.

"What about this report, Doctor, that you were born in Honolulu?" I asked him.

[1] Every Chinese child, at its birth, has a horoscope of eight characters: two for the year, two for the month, two for the day, and two for the hour of its birth; the Chinese hour being equivalent to two of ours, while their years have an intercalary month every three years. Even the smallest village in China has its necromancers, who supply the proper characters for the new-born child—when they are not otherwise provided—as well as the characters for marriages and deaths. These characters are always entered in the clan records, the records being printed from engraved blocks of wood, which, of themselves, supplement the records. Details such as this, however (and Chinese customs generally), shall not be allowed to encumber these pages except when absolutely essential.

[2] In this book the transliteration of Chinese names into English is made as simple as possible by omitting the hyphen and aspirate and giving each character the same lettering.

The Chinese write their names as we write ours in the telephone book; that is, the clan or family name (taken from the book of the hundred clans) comes first. After this generally come two descriptive names—descriptive to the clan name. The practice heretofore has been largely to write these two descriptive names with a hyphen, the second being uncapitalized. For example, John William Jones in Chinese, under the old style, would be Jones John-william. This, however, is merely a foreign affair and means nothing to the Chinese, and, since it likewise means nothing to us (except in a dictionary sense), in this book use of the hyphen is discontinued, and the names, both family and descriptive, are placed singly and spelled with a capital. In fact, the author would have preferred, if custom had allowed (as eventually it may), to run all the names together, Japanese fashion, as, Sunyatsen, instead of Sun Yat-sen, or, as we use it in this book, Sun Yat Sen. Sun's name is sometimes latinized to Sunyacius.

4

He smiled. Sun always smiles the smile of friendship when he speaks of his followers.

"It is true that the report was circulated. You see, some of my over-zealous followers thought that I could obtain protection from the American Government against the Manchus by claiming to have been born in Honolulu, where, in fact, I did live for many years. So, of their own accord, they circulated this report; but ah, no! Choy Hung . . . Choy Hung . . . that is the hamlet of my birth, and the birthplace of my immediate forebears. I say immediate forebears, for we have lived only a few generations in Choy Hung. The village of our ancestral temples is at Kung Kun, on the East River."

Choy Hung, as a birthplace for a child who wanted to become a reformer, was n't such a bad town. These small, open-air towns of Kwantung are very democratic, and boys grow up in a free-for-all way that develops independence of character. In the large Chinese cities the economic caste system (I do not mean social) is sometimes something of a hindrance to the development of a boy's democracy of character. If a boy's parents are able to send him to school, he may consider himself to be on the road to high scholarship and will not do any kind of manual labor. "Me no belong coolie," is an expression familiar to any

5

foreigner who has sojourned in China, for even the house-boy takes on this superior economic caste and will not do any sort of coolie labor when he is elevated to a house-boy station. To illustrate, I might mention a young underling writer in my office, who endured the privation of great cold during the Chinese New Year's interim because he would not degrade himself by making a fire, as he would thus be taking the place of the coolie who had gone home for the holidays. This young writer could write fifteen thousand Chinese ideographs with beautiful accuracy and yet hardly had the practical sense to make a fire in a modern stove, for he had always kept himself, and his precocious scholarship, so daintily away from any manual labor that he was helpless to attend to his own comfort. Poor chap!

From this idea of nonsense the boys in the Town of the Blue Valley were very free, for they all had some manual labor to do and naturally looked upon hard labor as being part of their daily life, beyond the routine of the temple school.

Again, Choy Hung was an advantageous birth-place for Sun Yat Sen because, about the time he was born, men of wealth, from Canton and Macao, began to establish there summer homes and places of outing and resort, on account of its picturesque location and its nearness to those large cities.

Hence from the comings and goings of these men the village folk had their imaginations quickened and their wits sharpened by dealings with the denizens of the cities.

More than this, Choy Hung was a wonderful birthplace because it was not far from the Kam Shing anchorage, the Harbor of Venus, the port of the Golden Star; Kam meaning gold, Shing meaning star. In that early time the Manchus generally did not allow foreigners to anchor on the Chinese-Macao side, nor at Canton; so the Harbor of Venus was set aside for them, being central to the three ports of Hong Kong, Canton, and Macao. Hence Kam Shing took on some reflected importance from these three large centers of commerce and population. The Town of the Blue Valley was only a brisk morning's walk from the Harbor of Venus, and about everything that happened in that harbor came to the waiting ears of the simple but gradually awakening people of Choy Hung.

"One of the earliest recollections that I have," Sun once narrated to me, "was the story that a dear old adopted auntie in our family told me. I was only a tiny boy, but this dear old auntie thought to entertain me by telling me about the Harbor of Venus. Oh! Then it seemed so very far away to me—that Harbor of the Golden Star

7

—although it was so very near! Auntie had lived
in the adjacent town of Shian Cha formerly, and
at Shian Cha they have an unrestricted view of the
waters of the Harbor of Venus. Well, auntie was
a good story-teller. She declared that dreadful
things were happening on those foreign ships and
that it was not safe to have them around; that the
foreigners were all rich men dressed in the queer-
est of clothes and that none of them wore a queue,
and that some of them had no hair on their heads,
at all, but lots of beard, and sometimes the beard
as red as fire. She had been told that when they
ate they put sharp knives up to their faces. She
further declared that one day she saw the smoke
rising from muskets, of which they made very free
use, much to her fear and perturbation. Ah, they
were a rash lot, those Ocean-men, and good little
Chinese boys would do well to stay away from
them.''

While the little lad did his share in the farm
labor after the hours in the temple school, his
mind was developing the set idea that if such a
fuss were made over the Ocean-men they must be
worth while to know. Sun Yat Sen is not a man
of many words. As I reflect, it seems strange to
me, the very few questions that he has ever asked
me. So I don't think that, as a boy, he went about
asking questions concerning the Ocean-men. I

8

do believe, however, that his imagination was much more fired by these tales of the Ocean-men than that of the average Chinese lad, and, that to him, even the manual labor of his child environment took on something of the uplift that eventually made him the Founder of the Chinese Republic. For he early realized that there was something beyond the glaze of the green- or red-tile roof; something more beautiful than ebony carvings or brilliant hanging scrolls or quaintly paneled lattices. However, Sun tells me that his first real information concerning the land of the Ocean-men came from a returned emigrant.

As regards these Chinese emigrants, returned from the gold-fields of America, it is known that the only demand for Chinese labor in America that we have ever allowed to be supplied was in the early days of California gold-fields. Then the demand was keen. Gold claims were staked out, men watching their precious holdings with guns in their hands to protect them; but there was no labor to be had for the panning out of the gold. A fabulous offer of wage failed to obtain laborers, so great was the distance from the large centers of American population to the new virgin land of gold. The American laborer, or white foreign laborer, of to-day became a gold-claim owner on the morrow. Sufficient immediate labor could not

9

be had at any price on the gold side of the American Continent, and Europe was too far away to supply this need in those early days of slow Atlantic and transcontinental travel. Therefore, in the dilemma, the American miners turned to China.

"Bring us over the Chinese at any price!" was their cry, with the result that, in short order, Chinese were being shanghaied, or otherwise brought to California by inducements little short of kidnapping. But, once in California, these Chinese received such fabulous wages that they were well satisfied with the fate that at first had seemed so cruel.

Then these emigrants—with their hoards of virgin gold nuggets, of five-, ten-, and twenty-dollar gold pieces, gold grains in leather pouches, such as had never before been seen in or about the Harbor of the Golden Star or Choy Hung—commenced to return to their homes.

"I met one of these when I was still very young," said the Reformer. "I stood in the door of the tea-house while he told the tale of his wanderings; of the great sea he had traversed for days and days, and then a fair land with mountains and water the same as in China, but with gold, oh, so much gold! But there were men—called men of red—and highwaymen; and they

10

would kill for the gold. Ah! this emigrant told me a story that I have remembered all my life,'' went on Sun Yat Sen. ''The emigrant declared that he always carried his gold in two parts; one very lightly concealed, so that when the highwaymen found it they would take it and go their way; while the other part, more deftly concealed, the emigrant would still have for himself. In our little Choy Hung this tale greatly interested us, for we, too, knew what pirates were. What impressed us most was the lesson that it pays to divide with the other man; for, as the emigrant went on to state, some of his comrades, who wished to save their all, were killed. It seemed to me as a lad that in this give-and-take world this particular emigrant had developed a particular philosophy which proved of practical advantage in a number of applications.''

With the waters of the Harbor of Venus and the Golden Star ever calling him to the Land of Gold and Adventure, little Sun Yat Sen from his earliest childhood was possessed by a yearning for the Overseas where he eventually planned to go; but there was an obstacle to his plans, and for years it seemed at times almost insurmountable. We shall learn what this was in subsequent sketches. As we were talking it over, I asked Sun Yat Sen:

"Did you never think of running off, of getting on one of those foreign ships and making your way over to America in spite of the opposition to it?"

"Ah, no," he responded. "No, I could never have thought of that because that would have been against my duty to my people."

In this response lies the philosophy of the Reformer. It was his loyalty and sense of duty to his "people" (who are now become the people of all China, by reason of his great leadership) that has made him the greatest of all living Chinese.

# II

BEFORE we go any further, we should know something of Kwantung and of the Cantonese people who, in their racial activity, gave Sun that resiliency of soul and agility of body that stood him in such good stead during the years of his wanderings about the world to accomplish the overthrow of the Manchus.

Kwantung, the southernmost of the eighteen provinces of China, is of itself a great and rich country with a population exceeding thirty millions. Canton, its capital and largest city, with over a million inhabitants, has taken its name from the English transliteration of the name of the province.

The Province of Kwantung is a fair and beautiful country, traversed by ranges of colorful mountains, drained by landscaped rivers, and skirted by an azure sea in a broken coast of purple heights and golden strands, along which are found many charming islands, picturesque with pagodas and bat-winged junks. The soil, although overworked by generations of farmers, is (with the aid of fer-

13

tilizers and intensive culture) rich in products of rice, tobacco, oil, silk, and tea. Then, there have always been many thriving manufactures in Kwantung. Most of our earlier imports from China came solely from this rich and sunny province of the South.

The Cantonese are a very intelligent and active people, as the world knows from having used their products for many years. Even the firecrackers which delighted our small boys in America before the advent of the Sane Fourth came from that fair land.

It is an open-air country, with summer most of the year, with a cool, vital tang in the air corresponding to our winter months, thus removing much of the sluggishness that generally obtains in warm climates.

Canton is the most progressive of Chinese cities, not only because it is in the midst of things (Hong Kong being only seventy-eight miles away, and Macao approximately half as far), but particularly because of its large number of returned emigrants, who have taken on something of American ways after their residence in America. Indeed, a great proportion of the Chinese who live, and have lived, in America came from Kwantung, largely because, in the California gold days, as already noted, it was cheaper and more conveni-

14

ent to bring labor from this land of low wage than from other places, the great shipping center of Hong Kong offering particular facilities for economical and rapid transportation of these Chinese steerage passengers.

The Cantonese, as a race, are lively and sociable and of marked intelligence. As a tropical people they are not always as robust and strong in physique as their brothers of the North; but what they lack in this regard they make up in a suppleness and agility of limb that plays to advantage in any hard labor they undertake.

Kwantung, particularly in the Choy Hung section, offers a climate that favors physical development. Although Choy Hung lies in the tropics, it has an invigorating winter period, and once in a lifetime there may be frost or a little light flaking of snow. The city of Canton, forty miles from Choy Hung, is the only metropolis near the seacoast and at sea-level in the tropics where there is frost. Sun Yat Sen is one of the few leaders who were born and brought up in the tropics, and much of the vigor and strength shown by him in his long effort to overthrow the Manchus came not from the tonic of climatic influences but rather from the invigorating surroundings of his rude rural life and from the happiness of a domestic circle within whose tranquillity were built up

15

those nerve-centers that were to stand him in such good stead in the hard and adventurous life to come.

The Cantonese are a courageous, self-reliant, and hardy race. They have always been very patriotic and intensely Chinese, in spite of their comparative isolation from the great centers of Middle and Northern China. They have produced scholars of great distinction and, as a race, have constituted as great a protection to the Middle Kingdom on the south as the Great Wall itself on the north. They use a language highly developed in its phonetics, the Cantonese possessing one more tone than the Mandarin, thus making five tones. In the arts and crafts they have been known as masters from the earlier periods and are, altogether, a people second to none in general Chinese intelligence and racial tenacity.

Among the Chinese, their women are noted for their beauty and virtue, and since they are of a handsome brunette type, their complexion takes on a tone of olive rather than the lighter ivory shade observed among the Chinese women of the North.

The life of the Cantonese masses is easier than that of many other Chinese, for they are an open-air people and enjoy the ease that goes with open-air life. They need no heating fuel nor heavy winter garments. The farmers, particularly in such fertile spots as the Blue Valley, lead a life much easier than does the Northern Chinese farmer, for nature assists him more freely in his labors. Rice is the principal Kwantung crop and the *sine qua non* of their existence. Fruits of many varieties—even the banana—are cultivated, and the succulent lichi nut of Canton (known wherever there is a Chinese emigrant) is widely renowned. Sugar-cane grows abundantly, but Sun Yat Sen told me that his family found it to be a very hard crop on the overworked soil, and that in Choy Hung but little sugar is produced, although elsewhere in the province it is a substantial crop.

Down along the tide-waters an abundance of fish can be had, but in Choy Hung what fish was used was brought from the near-by towns on the tide-water.

Thus Kwantung as a whole we find to be a land of great attraction, that little part in which we are most interested participating in the general prosperity that belonged to the whole provincial region.

All Cantonese are very proud of being Cantonese, and no doubt the "native son" idea of the province did much to sustain Sun in his thirty years of effort toward the founding of the Republic. There was hardly a Cantonese abroad that did not support his cause.

Mutual help and coöperation are habits with them, and the result is seen in the prosperity of Cantonese merchants all over the world, the principal department-stores here in Shanghai being developed and run by Cantonese capital and managers.

Thus it would seem that Sun was very fortunate in being born a Cantonese, for his political activity could find a greater support in Canton than in many other parts of China. The Cantonese were rich and progressive, and from the broadening influence of their migrations to America they had taken on a certain push of political temperament that only needed the leverage of Sun's leadership to put it in action. Most of the Dare-to-Dies came from Kwantung, although this is perhaps more a matter of Sun's personal leadership than otherwise.

## III

### THE FATHER OF THE STRAIGHT WAY

SUN YAT SEN'S father once had the wander-lust, and early in his youth had gone to Macao —the "Goddess Bight"—thirty miles away, as an apprentice, to learn the tailoring trade.

When a Choy Hung lad obtained a job in Macao he rarely returned to remain permanently in the hamlet of the Blue Valley, for the Portuguese, by their close affiliation with the Chinese, adapted their western civilization to accommodate all the pleasures and vices known to the Chinese; and even a "makie learnie pidgin" boy had his share in the round of pleasures that the Lusitanians played to the allurement of the Chinese, for they wanted the poor Chinese for their labor, and the rich Chinese for their capital. The struggling, adventurous early Lusitanians had brought from the Tagus little save the caravels in which they traveled to the land of spice and silk and jade. For the most part, they came to China empty-handed as beggars, and thus, from the beginning, realized their dependence upon the bounty of Chinese labor, and the prodigality of the Chinese capitalists.

To allure this bounty and prodigality, the Portuguese went to great pains to make Macao the Mecca of the Chinese pleasure-seeker, be he rich or poor, and well might the Chinese of all classes declare, as they made the round of Macao's pleasures,

> If e'er there was a Heaven of bliss—
> It is this! it is this! it is this!

Yes, they made Macao a town of wild and extravagant pleasures, and from the very beginning seemed to have had this end in view. Selecting a site on the meandering tropical coast (noted for its beauty among the Chinese from its earliest days), they raised those walls of yellow, pink, and blue that shone in the glory of Kwantung's sun, like gems half hidden in the green of the Praya Grande, where the skirt of the sea showed the deepest purple of its edge. They established, on a grand and extravagant scale, that master lure to the Chinese sybarite, the gambling-place, and to its wild allurements added wholesale a choice of Bacchanalian dissipations, rivaling, in their ensemble, the orgies of a Pompeian festival. Wickedness throve because it had the support of piety, throve because it was a passive part of the prayers of the church, which depended largely for its living upon the profits of those vices against which it preached.

It was wicked, but it was beautiful. Ah! those blue and pink and yellow walls! A color for each of the master vices, opium, lewd women, and gambling; those master vices that mean to the Chinese, in the unrestraint of his ancient life, a natural pleasure, that he who has the means buys as easily as plucking a flower, and as naturally as the bee sucking honey from the heart of an orchid.

Yes, blue and pink and yellow walls, with flowers and singing birds upon them, and yet, eventually, a noisome prison for so many of those peasant lads from the hamlets like Choy Hung, who had finally come down to the dregs of the cup of pleasure they sought at any price; and, beyond those walls of color, the songs from the flower-boats; the laughter of the pleasure-seekers in the balmy air; the rich and merry festivals, all making a picture in which Macao—swung from the ever summer sky of the Southern Cross like a gaudy lantern, garish by day but tauntingly beautiful as it gleamed out through the midnight hours —had its background in those villages of the Blue Valleys, those hamlets of lowly yet honest toil, of precarious privations and sacrifice, and yet with a compensation for every hour of labor.

When Sun Yat Sen told me about his father's

21

journey and sojourn in Macao, I forecast the usual
acceptance of the snares of Macao. For the elder
Sun, like all Chinese, loved pleasure, and as he
was assured of a position as a tailor's apprentice,
it seemed inevitable to me that he should remain
in that city of seduction like the great majority
that passed that way.

"And your father, how long did he remain in
Macao?" I asked.

"Not very long, as I remember; for he became
homesick and yearned for his Choy Hung. He
was homesick because his duty was at home."

"Homesick? Duty?" thought I. "What Chinese lad could be homesick in such a town as Macao?"

" 'Homesick' and 'duty.' Yes," I reflected,
"here was another foundation-stone in the character of the Reformer. His father preferred the
duty of family associations rather than the pleasures of Macao, and with such sense of duty and
decency, can we wonder when the boy turns from
the colored lights of Macao and follows down the
sorghum brakes that line the waters beyond Macao, and lead back to the rude and hard simplicity
of his hamlet life, dearer to him than all the
pleasures that he had left behind!"

The elder Sun did not come back from the City
of Pleasure like the Prodigal Son. He had done

well in Macao. He had performed his duty there, and came back to Blue Valley with something of saved money and a knowledge of the tailor trade, which, if need be, he could use to advantage in supplementing his work in the rice-paddies, the bean and cotton fields.

To one who knows the looseness of Chinese morals, this clean home-coming was commendable and remarkable. The red pleasure lights showing out on the moon-lit waters of the Praya Grande were as tiny fireflies in their influence on this youth who was to become the father of one of the greatest reformers of all time. He was made of a stuff that made pure home life a model of duty and ambition. Not for this duty-loving youth were the lascivious passion-songs of the flower-boats, the gilded blandishments of the gaming-houses, and the thick, sweet vapor of the opium couch. With no God, and with no background of morality for a conscience, from his sheer personal respect he had turned away from that midst of smiling, black-haired sirens, the lewd flower-girls, and the unctuous entertainers, and had come back to the bosom of his rude home, clean and whole-some, with his brow held high, to become the pro-genitor of a family in which, through one single member, the leadership of a great part of the world would eventually be involved.

23

"I think that your father was wonderful," I declared.

"Wonderful? Well, he was good. He had the respect of his family and of his fellow-men."

With this remark a vision flashed before me. . . . Macao as I last saw it, with its purple hills, its gay edge of water, and a dozen colors—of man's making—to mingle with the deeper tones of God's own nature.

Then, in the vision, I saw the night fall, and only the red lights of the flower-boats showing, and in the darkness came the wail of the singsong girls as they were driven out into the gloom, emblematic of the decay of beautiful Macao—a fair city, but going down with the cancer of vice to a certain doom. A city—and a youth—and of the two the youth had proved stronger than the whole city, for from his flesh and conscience came the mastery of a self-control that eventually, through his issue, would bring a leadership—a leadership for the better things of life for a whole race.

I think that much of Sun Yat Sen's great moral force came to him as an inheritance from that father who, without knowledge of the precepts of the true God, from the decent sense of his own, fine nature, gave up his easy task of making garments for pleasure-seekers to return to the rude, hard labor in the stony fields of Blue Valley.

There was even some of this shop congeniality in the little town of
Blue Valley.

"Dr. Sun had given me a picture of his family with his mother as the central figure"
(Page 25).

# IV

## THE MOTHER WITH THE BOUND FEET

DR. SUN had given me a picture of his family with his mother as a central figure. The picture showed his mother, well advanced in years, but with a dignity and softness of expression that indicated that she was a lady of beauty in her youth. Advancing years, according to the picture, had taken much of that luxurious hair which distinguishes Cantonese women, the Chinese idea of hair-dressing being the opposite of ours. (Our American ladies dress their hair to show as much of it as possible; Chinese ladies dress theirs to show as little as possible, dressing it down into a shining, close-fitting helmet, plastered to the skull.) The picture shows her to have been a graceful and dignified lady, the features indicating great force of womanly character. She shows a slight tapering of the chin, the thin line of eyebrow well arched, and with hardly any of those lines and shadows that mark the faces of women in their old age. "A lovely old lady," is what one would declare on looking at her picture.

25

But there was one thing that bothered me in this picture: the tiny little feet peeping out from beneath the silken skirt of that dear old lady seated in the midst of the eleven members of her family! I don't know why, but it shocked me to think that the Reformer's mother should have had "squeezed" feet.

"Perhaps the picture misleads me," thought I. "Perhaps the supposed tiny feet are merely the points of shoes that fit normal feet."

As I walked from Hongkew over to the Suns' house in the French Concession that morning, I reflected, as never before, on this strange custom of the Chinese.

Undoubtedly this severe custom arose and flourished through the desire of the Chinese to mark their women by such indubitable signs of identity as to make impossible any mistakes of their race. The Manchu did not bind the feet of his women. The Mandarin might or might not, as he desired, consider any woman whose feet were unbound as of other race than Chinese. The Manchus were held by the most solemn pledges to respect Chinese womanhood, and intermarriage was forbidden. But there had to be a way of fixing identity; and the passport of the Chinese woman was her bound feet, just as the passport of the Chinese man was his queue. The woman with the bound feet had a dignity all her own. She was eligible as a "number one" wife and free from concubinage. What mattered to her the dread, long years of suffering to accomplish the maiming of her feet, if at the end she arrived at the full franchise of eligibility to first marital rights?

Now, it is not polite to make inquiries concerning the family of a Chinese, and it seemed to me that, despite my close companionship with Sun Yat Sen, it would be hard to obtain in any courteous way information as to whether or not the mother of the great Reformer had bound feet. To ask straight out, "Doctor, did your mother have bound feet?" would be more indecorous than to ask of an American or English friend of high dignity and propriety, "Say, did your deceased mother lace tightly?"

However, I thought, finally, of a way of obtaining the information without running the risk of hurting Sun's feelings.

I had the picture with me. It was one taken from a book that Sun had given me, a copper-plate illustration, and perhaps the only one now in existence.

I first asked Sun some general questions concerning the family group, who they were and so forth, and finally, pointing to his mother's picture, I said:

27

"It is a very nice gown, and the shoes are very small and dainty."

"Yes," declared Sun in a very matter-of-fact tone, "my mother, as Chinese, of course, had bound feet."

He looked at the picture tenderly, and then added:

"One reason why we tolerated the custom so long was out of respect to our mothers." The Reformer's voice grew softer as he spoke of his mother, her of the bound feet.

Sun Yat Sen's father wore the queue, and his mother had bound feet; they were true Chinese, proud of the traditions of their race, happy in the strength of their family circle, and they lived a life of devotion to each other.

To the support of this Chinese good mother of the bound feet, ever stood two other good Chinese women, likewise, of course, with bound feet.

These two women were widows. They had married the two next younger brothers of Sun Yat Sen's father. Just how and when and where they were widowed, they did not know; but they did know why. They ever remembered that fatal day when the two brothers stood before them in their best garments for that long journey from which they would never return. They answered the supplications and tears of their wives with words of encouragement and endearment, and voiced their hopes for an early and safe return.

These two brothers were going to the Land of Gold. They were among the very first in the whole region of the Harbor of Venus to undertake voluntarily the long and precarious voyage to America. So they sailed away from the waters of the Golden Star to bring back gold to the loved ones at home, gold that their strong arms were to take from the mountains of California.

Oh, how long and devotedly those two women waited for news from the departed! No word came. Months and years passed. Finally hope was abandoned, and the family circle in Blue Valley knew that the two wanderers must have perished. Nothing of their tragic fate was ever given in detail. It was only known that one had perished on the ship "somewhere beyond Shanghai," and that the other had "died in the gold-fields of California."

Sun Yat Sen's father, as the elder brother of each of the two vanished men, took the two widows into his home according to Chinese custom. Thus these two lone women, still yearning for the loved ones who would never return, became part of the family circle presided over by the Leader's mother. One of them was the auntie who, we recall, advised Sun as a lad to be a good little boy and stay away from the Océan-men.

When the news of the death of the two adventurous brothers was finally and reluctantly accepted, it was agreed by the common assent of the whole family circle that none of the children should ever be allowed to go forth to California, that land of peril. Hence young Sun's ambitions in that regard were severely suppressed. The folly of leaving his good home in Blue Valley to face enemies in the Ocean-men's world was ever pointed out to him.

The mother and the two widows, who were daily, in their tearful sorrow, paying the price of the temerity of their venturesome husbands, supported the elder Sun with all their hearts when he voiced again and again his protest against the foolhardiness of going to the Land of Vanished Men. After repeated admonitions, at length, he complacently surveyed the family circle, solaced in the thought that the Ocean-men's enticement would no longer lure added members from its midst.

Ah, good old father with the queue, and dear, good women of the bound feet, little did ye dream that the tiny, silent lad in the corner would, in spite of the warnings of the past, eventually seek out, in the land of the Ocean-men, an inspiration that would shake great China loose from the tyranny of centuries!

In the meantime, the obstacle of family objection was there, and the obedient little lad, having no God to pray to, reflected in his young heart upon the bitterness of fate.

But he felt that some time he would go to the perilous land of the Ocean-men, and safely brave its dangers; and that, somehow, a way would be found to obtain the consent of the whole family circle for this, his Great Adventure.

## V

### THE DESCENDANT OF LEISURE IMMORTAL

THE family name Sun means a descendant, and the first of Sun's given names, Yat, means leisure, the name being given to him Chinese fashion, with the idea that he should hold up the leisurely easy life as one of his maxims in life.

The other name, Sen, means immortal, so that, a transliteration of the name Sun Yat Sen, "The Descendant of Leisure Immortal" would be about as clear as any other; to the same end was also added the school name Wen, meaning learned.

Nearly every one knows now (as has been already noted) that the Chinese place their family names as we place ours in the telephone book; that is, the family name, as the more important, comes first. It is also generally known that the Chinese, instead of giving their children some set name that varies from generation to generation in its style, as do we, give them names which imply qualities which they hope their children will

enjoy or at least emulate. We have something of
this method when we find an American boy called
Loyal, the parents' idea being that the boy should
ever remember loyalty because of his name: or,
in the case of a girl named Grace, the thoughtful
parents believe that, in bestowing this name upon
the little one they are giving her an incentive to
be gracious. Among the Chinese, to make this
method partake of a certain definiteness, sometimes the village schoolmaster takes a hand in
the bestowing of these given names, expressing
qualifications.

Those who had a hand in naming Sun conceived in the rich imagery of the ideographs that
they were giving him a name that implied ease
and leisure, into which his undying diligence would
eventually reflect great credit upon his family, the
family of the "grandsons" or "descendants."

The name Sun Yat Sen has the advantage of
being easily remembered by foreigners, particularly by those who speak English, since it is al-
literative and rhythmic, with none of the aspirates
or double consonants that are so confusing to the
person unacquainted with the transliteration of
Chinese into English or other tongues. It might
be well to note here that the Reformer is more
generally known among Chinese as Sun Wen, and
in this regard reference is made to the way he

has signed his name on the lateral scroll dedicated to the author.

The names Sun Yat Sen and Sun Wen to the Chinese are very good "joss," for these names have that necessary imagery and mental suggestion that, to use the Chinese expression, "cover everything"; meaning that the name is well fashioned, and filled with that significance for which Chinese look in names, in a way hard to understand for those not familiar with the Chinese mind.

When Sun was finally acknowledged as the leader of the anti-Manchu movement, far from showing any jealousy, his followers would say, with a play on the ideographs of his name: "It is proper for a Sun"—meaning descendant—"to take care of the interests of the whole family. Dr. Sun, therefore, by his name, is entitled to the guardianship of the family property of the people"; which seems rather far-fetched from our Occidental viewpoint, but which is perfectly clear to the Chinese method of expression.

This name, which has long since become a household name the world over, may thus literally be considered as meaning Mr. Leisure and Immortality, belonging to the family called Descendant. One part of the prophecy of the name has already

34

come true, that of being an Immortal, for surely the great Leader's name will be known as long as history itself survives.

However, the "leisure" prophecy of the name is unfulfilled, and probably always will be, as I doubt if there ever has been a man more eternally active and in the enjoyment of less leisure than Sun Yat Sen; but fitting the rule the other way, in the amiable, indulgent manner with which the Chinese regard everything pertaining to their language, we may say that the prophecy has come true in the sense that Sun Yat Sen is Mr. Leisure in the way he achieves an immortal name, for he is, indeed, leisurely and sure in his methods, and I doubt if he has ever done anything in his whole thinking life that has not been preceded by something of deliberation. Of the thousands of questions I have asked him, I know that he has answered none upon which he has not thought, and I have, at times, become fidgety in waiting, during a suspensive period, for an answer. It is this sort of leisurely mentality that always speaks the truth, and I doubt if a man ever lived who was more painstakingly truthful than is Sun Yat Sen.

Just as at home, an easily pronounced and immediately remembered name is of great advantage to a man starting out in public life, so in

China and abroad I think that Sun's cheerful and attractive name has been of at least some small advantage to him.

There was, likewise, a disadvantage among the Chinese as regards his surname. It seems remarkable that Sun Yat Sen, belonging as he did to one of the smallest tribal divisions, ever obtained the great following that he has. For, with the Chinese, from a viewpoint of public popularity, it is considered desirable to belong to one of the more numerous families; the greater the family the more the relatives and the more the tribal representation and consequent influence. All Chinese consider themselves to be more or less related if they have the same family name. With us when John Smith is introduced to a man named Henry Smith he does not consider that there is any relationship and regards the similarity of name as a mere coincidence. But if a Chinese of the family name of Li is introduced to another of the same family name he will presumably declare:

"Ah, it is a pleasure to meet a new-found relative, for I perceive that we have the same ancestors."

There are few family names in China, and all family names must have one syllable only. The Lis, the Wongs, the Hwangs, the Lums, the Chuns, and the Chongs make up some of the very large

Sun's childhood knew only the sleepy Old China of yesterday, of which this pagoda scene is emblematic.

Sun ever conceived in his thirty years of revolutionary disappointments a new China whose railroads would be greater even than the Great Wall of China, whose tiny outline is seen on the mountain above.

林百克先生庋

天下為公

孫文

"... the Reformer is more generally known among the Chinese as Sun Wen, and in this regard reference is made to the way he has signed his name on the lateral scroll dedicated to the author" (Page 34). The original of this scroll is five feet wide. Of the four characters, the first, *Tien*, means "heaven," the second, *Shia*, "beneath," the third, *Wei*, "for," and the fourth, *Gong*, "patriotic." A translation of this *pien* or lateral scroll is, "All nations should be the opposite of selfishness," which may be liberally rendered, "Brotherhood of all nations." The Reformer's signature appears in the left lower corner above his private seal, which is in the seal characters (Chuan). The inscription to the author appears at the right, the author's name in the imagery of the Chinese language being "Mr. Lim of the Hundred Victories," although the author must confess that unfortunately the "hundred victories" are merely imaginative.

tribal families in China, and it is considered to be something of a privilege to belong to these larger tribal families. It expands a man's life, and is an admittance to the sort of tribal freemasonry that prevails in the family tribe system of China. Names mean a great deal more in China than in America or Europe, particularly since the law of marital relations prohibits intermarriage between persons of the same family name.

The original village of the Sun Family, as has already been noted, was not in Choy Hung; a part had outgrown the original village and migrated from it. These migrations are not uncommon in China. Our own family unity is far less constant and continued than that of the Chinese. Migrations with us generally mean a scattering of the family. The Chinese family as a coöperative institution always holds together, as regards the attachment not only to father and mother but to the grandparents and even collaterals. Famine, pirates, war, and pestilence are the more ordinary causes of migration. When a migration takes place, it is like a movement of a camp of Indians, the whole family proceeding to their new place of abode in a solid company. No member is left behind. This attachment to family has contributed, perhaps as much as anything else to hold the Chinese to the mold of their political stagnation.

As long as a family keeps together, each member being merely a link in the chain, no link can be made the nucleus of a new force.

As regards family customs, it seems peculiar to us that the Chinese girls of a village can never marry the boys of that village. The purpose of this law was to strengthen the blood of the people and avoid the possibility of incestuous relation. In Europe and in some of the States of America, even cousins may marry, but in China so strict is the control of law and custom in this respect that, as noted, even Chinese of the same surname may not intermarry. For example, Miss Wong, whose family has lived in Peking for half a thousand years, cannot marry Mr. Wong of Canton, although it is accepted that neither family has ever seen anything of the other from time immemorial. Their surnames, from the Chinese viewpoint, are conclusive proof that at one time both had a common origin.

The village of the Blue Valley not being a Sun village—that is, its inhabitants not being all Suns, and the surname not running through the entire village, as is frequently the case in Chinese towns —Sun's parents might have chosen a wife for him from among some of the girls in the village of his birth. However, it happened eventually that his boyhood wife was selected for him from a neigh-

38

boring town, as is indicated in the chapter on "Domestic Relations."

In passing, we might state that one reason why the girl is not so welcome as the boy in the Chinese family is because so many of the girls are so utterly lost to their families by being required, under this marriage custom, to marry into a family far distant from that of their parents, another reason being that custom does not allow her to perform the ancestral rites.

The Sun family was fortunate in the first respect, for the valleys about abounded in villages, and the Sun girls could enjoy more association with their own families than in other more thinly populated parts of China.

The family of the "descendants" and the "grandsons," although not original settlers of Choy Hung, were none the less of importance in the town as far as the little circle of the hundred families of the town went. The Suns had one of the roomiest homes in Choy Hung even at the time of the Reformer's birth. This home, however, was razed some thirty-five years ago to make way for a much larger and more attractive building, as will be seen in the lower left corner of our illustration. I here express my thanks to Dr. Sun's son for these pictures. The newer building was built by Sun Yat Sen's mother with money given her by Da Ko,[1] the elder brother, of whom we shall hear much as we go along.

The Suns were a prominent family in the village of Blue Valley, particularly in the correctness of their Chinese life. They were thoroughly orthodox in their adherence to Chinese customs. They prostrated themselves before the village idol and worshiped the Son of Heaven.

There was little in their environment to lead them out of the rut of their correct Chinese life, and so the family of the "descendants" in Blue Valley lived like millions of other Chinese families, distinguished, however, by a rugged, wholesome family affection and sense of duty to their fellow-men that eventually was to crystallize itself into a leadership beyond the circle of the family.

[1] Da means great, or in this connection elder; and Ko means brother. In the subsequent chapter entitled "My Brother Da Ko" the word "Brother" is surplusage but is used for descriptive purpose.

# VI

WHAT did your family call you when you were a boy?"

A smile flitted over Sun's face, with a tender expression as he harked back to the family circle in which the places were now nearly all vacant.

"They call me Wen." (Wen means Literature, Education, or Civil Scholar.)

Considering the fact that Sun always led his classes in every institution he attended, whether at home or abroad, even graduating with first honors in the Hong Kong Medical College, it would seem that he was, indeed, entitled to the appellation of Civil Scholar.

"What was it that you most wanted as a boy, not at school but at play?"

The answer came quickly without the usual long reflection.

"A strange question," he declared. "I have reflected frequently myself upon that great childhood's desire of mine. . . . I wanted a bird. A real *singing* bird."

I myself meditated upon the longing of a Chi-

41

nese farm lad for a singing bird. Singing birds are not so common in the farm fields and pasture meadows of China as in America. Chinese farmers have no time for snaring birds or making cages for them. That is the business of the bird-trainer and the cage-maker. But to those who can afford to buy birds, China is a wonderful realm of bird melody. Oh, what wonderful songs the Chinese teach their birds! But that is for the rich man of the city, not for the plowboy of the Blue Valley fields.

I did not ask Sun if he ever got his bird, for he was silent, and silence is with Sun a negative answer. I know he never got it, and I know he never asked for it. He wanted a bird, one of the singing kind, yet, with all his longing, never asked for it because it was not "custom" for a boy to have a singing bird in the hard-worked midst of Blue Valley.

With this esthetic longing for a bird, the lad's mind held a great love for all the rude sports in which the boys of his town indulged. He loved these sports in spite of the continued admonitions of his teacher that "all sports are a waste of time."

Kite-flying was a delight to Wen. The Chinese have developed kite-flying to a science. They have their musical kites by which a vibration is

42

struck on a tight-drawn wire or strip of bamboo across the kite. With a dozen huge musical kites in the air, a most remarkable assembling of sounds is heard, which, if not musical to our ears, is, at all events, satisfying to the Chinese lad. The pyrotechnic kite, by which firecrackers were set off in mid-air by means of lighted punk attached to the kite, was another delight. The Chinese have, from time immemorial, manufactured giant firecrackers, of which the first terrific explosion drives the remainder of the load high into the air, where there is another loud explosion. This double-barreled onslaught is presumed by the ignorant to frighten away the evil spirits, both from the earth and from the air above. Even little Choy Hung had its share in this superstitious belief.

There were other sports into which Wen entered heartily, such as kicking feathers (similar to our shuttlecock), leapfrogging, the game of stick-measuring, and sugar-cane chopping. The game of stick-measuring consisted in batting one stick with another, the smaller stick being caught in the tail of the lad's gown. If he caught it, he, in turn, became the batter, and the victory in the game was measured in the batting-distance from the home plate.

Sugar-cane chopping involved something of a

gamble. The stick of sugar-cane was held upright, and was released as it fell, the player striking at it with a heavy knife, cutting off as large a piece as he could before it reached the ground. The victory went to the one who succeeded in cutting off the largest slice.

I remember that I tried a little humor on Sun when he told me about this sugar-cane chopping game.

"Judging from the way you cut into the Manchus, you were very dexterous at this sugar-cane chopping game, were you not?"

Sun smiled, and I added, "It was a game of vinegar and not sugar with the Manchus, wasn't it?"

We both laughed, and for a time the smile of amusement shone on Sun's face.

Little Wen also loved top-spinning and followed the other games that came in rotation, as with us.

There was no chance to make money in a sort of half-play way as with the American boys of his generation such as peddling papers, catching fish, or gathering up junk to sell to the junk-dealer; all this child work-play was denied him, for if there was the smallest piece of cash to be had it was not for the children. On the rare occasions that a Blue Valley boy did obtain a small piece of copper—say the twentieth of an Amer-

Water-buffalo at primitive irrigation plant.

The Chinese farmer gets wonderful results even from the crudest equipment. It was in scenes such as the above that Wen passed his "hard-worked but happy childhood" (Page 46).

"Just another of the tens of thousands of Chinese Sleepy Hollows"
(Page 3).

Birthplace of Sun Yat Sen, the house wherein he was born having
been razed to make way for the present large house seen in the
left-hand corner (Page 39).

ican cent—he would probably treasure it by putting it aside, carefully wrapped in a piece of red paper. I doubt, however, if Wen would have gone into the money play-work game at all, for, on the theory that the "child is father to the man," I think that his indifference to money would have made him a poor competitor in such boyish attempts at capitalism.

The play periods of the day were short and infrequent, for, like all Chinese boys, he had a muddled, puzzled school-day seven times a week in which he had to learn the Thousand-Character Classic and the Trimetrical Primer, together with a mass of ideographs concerning the six kinds of grains, the five kinds of virtues; the whole hodge-podge seasoned with allusions to the powers of the heaven, sea, and land in a most overwhelming confusion.

Like all Chinese boys, he learned to look forward to the feast-days, for they were events of great family and village jollification, especially the long period of the New Year's celebration, the only really long holiday the Chinese have; with no Christmas or other Christian holiday, no Sunday, and no birthday of the American sort, it is no wonder that Wen, when he finally arrived at Honolulu at the age of thirteen, entered most heartily into the bigger play life of the Ocean-men, as is suggested in one of the following chapters.

However, with seven days of school, and with chore work for every one of these days in addition, Wen throve in the open air and wholesome surroundings. Sun and I spent a whole day talking over his Blue Valley boyhood; and it was, indeed, a very cheerful day, and far different from those many other days in which we discussed the periods where disappointment, bitterness, and the tragedy of great adventures filled every hour of our meeting. My impression of Sun's first thirteen years of life (all passed within a radius of a couple of miles of the village temple of Blue Valley) was that he had a hard-worked but happy childhood. He told me that there was always novelty for him in this early life, even in the dull routine of the hamlet of Blue Valley. In fact, I detected a wistful look coming over his face as we discussed the old Blue Valley homestead of that early day; and in this wistful look Sun seemed to say to me: "I did not want to be a leader. The perils and dangers of revolutionary life are not to my liking. I did not want to be the instrument of a great political collapse and responsible for the torrent of blood which it caused. I wanted to be happy and contented, just as I was in my boyhood in Blue Valley. But duty decreed otherwise."

I was so interested in Sun's boyhood that we went into the details of food, lodging, and clothing, all of which still stood out very clearly in Sun's memory. His food was the wholesome and fresh but rude product of the farm. Every member had some sort of an individual bed, something rare for Chinese in other parts of China. There were frequent changes of raiment, although much clothing was not needed in that warm climate of the South. Wen, as a matter of dignity, gave up going barefoot during his school hours and ceremoniously put on shoes with felt soles when he made ready for the temple school.

"What kind of a pillow did you use when you were a little fellow, Doctor?" I asked, since the terrific Chinese pillows of brick and crockery have always excited my interest.

The doctor smiled.

"I early learned to prefer a pillow made of a bag filled with beans. It was not as uncomfortable as a brick covered with cloth, nor as soft as a pillow of tea-leaves; so, as a lad, I thought I would strike a happy medium, a sort of 'middle of the road' adaptation."

Then we laughed, and our laughter increased

47

when I declared, "Now I know why the Empress Dowager hunted you about the whole world with a price on your head; you did not follow your 'middle of the road' theory when it came to the Manchus."

"When were your meal-times back on the farm?" I asked.

"As soon as we got up at dawn those of us who had to do the hard work of the fields would take a strengthening repast, but the rest of us would only take the regular two Cantonese meals of the day, one about nine in the morning and the other about four in the afternoon, the exact hour depending upon the convenience of those concerned."

"Was there anything to develop ambition in Choy Hung?"

"My mother was good; my father was good; and to obtain the respect of the family circle, an ambition to do my very best was always present, for there was a goodness that prevailed in our midst in spite of the ancient conditions which beclouded it. Of course, it was a goodness that looked backward rather than forward for its models, but it was a goodness that spelled morality in personal life. My mother wanted me to enjoy the happiness that went with the respect of the family circle, and in the village midst."

48

Sun spoke the word "mother" so tenderly that I sensed he was again thinking deep into the happiness of those early years, and of a mother who (as we shall see in a subsequent sketch) taught him that all life ended in death.

With all the superstition, however, of China's ancient world holding her down, the soul-strength of Sun's mother made her son good. I am sure that even Sun's genius of leadership would never have held out its reins of sympathy to the world of China's sorrow, had it not been for that mother who was good, and who yet believed that life ended with death.

No religion is greater than truth, and no influence is greater than that of a good mother.

# VII

WEN AND THE "SAN TSE CHIN"
(THREE-SYLLABLE CLASSIC)

FOR many centuries Chinese boys have stood with their faces to the walls of village temple schools and, under the threat of the whip of the schoolmaster, have recited in loud voices the three-word classic. They did not know what the recitation meant. It was a philosopher puzzle, which even the mature and learned would have to discuss before they could settle upon any given meaning.

But it was considered the only sure way of Chinese learning; for it was thought to teach filial affection, brotherly kindness, respectfulness, faithfulness, diligence, and benevolence. What more could one ask for in the realm of erudition?

Its system had been followed for a millennium. All great Chinese scholars had entered the Gate of Wisdom with a singsong recital of its mysteries. Therefore it was good, and all Chinese school lads must know the "San Tse Chin" by heart. The scholars were not divided into classes. No effort was made to standardize the instruction. Each lad made up a class to himself.

Sun, every day in the lunar month (the Chinese have no weeks), went to the village temple school to shout out with the rest the senseless repetition of the three-syllable classic, and write interminably long weary pages in the copy-books.[1]

Wen's young mind awakened to the nonsense of the instruction. He stood it for a long time, then rebelled.

"I do not understand. There is no reason in this singsong. Why should I learn it?"

The schoolmaster stood aghast. He reached for his bamboo rod, balanced it deftly in his hand. Then his arm dropped, for he had bethought himself. Wen was the best reciter in the whole school, and hence a beating would set no good example. Besides, Wen's father was a village elder, and perhaps an exception might be made in this case. The teacher, still threatening with the rod, however, cried out fiercely:

"What! You rebel against the classics?"

"No, I do not rebel against the classics. But why should I sing out this stuff day after day when I do not know what it means?"

"This is contumely against the learning of the

[1] A very literal translation of the first verses of the "San Tse Chin" will be found in the chapter, "Yamen Running to a Town of Ignorance."

wisdom of the ancients,'' declared the teacher fiercely.

''But I am taught to read, and I do not understand what I have learned to read,'' returned the recalcitrant youth.

The teacher was puzzled. Wen was making better progress than any other pupil in his class. Therefore, Wen should be pleased with his opportunity to learn the wisdom of the ancients.

''Will you not, please, help me to know the reason of what I am learning?'' pleaded the youngster.

The teacher's heart yielded. Yes, this was an exceptional case. The boy further explained to his teacher that there was a reason for everything else in the world; why, therefore, should the ideographs be so without meaning?

The teacher could not answer; but there was a friendliness that grew up from the lad's rebellion, and Wen, out of respect for his teacher, went heartily into the reasonless study of the classics and learned them in such wise that the teaching in the village temple school became the foundation of his scholarship, without which he could never have become the leader of the people.

But all the time that he worked so diligently at the classics, this thought echoed out in the sing-song of the classroom.

"There must be a reason even for the classics. Some day I shall find it."

In vain do we search the biographies of the world's reformers to find a parallel to this helplessness of the childhood of the Chinese Leader.

Other leaders have had something or some one, even in their childhood, upon which to shape the course of their youth for the future. Wen, the first pupil in the rude and noisy Blue Valley school, had no one and nothing to point as a guide toward the future. All went backward, nothing forward. All was in a background as black as the night, made blacker still by the dim and distant glow of those stars that his teacher referred to in quoting the wisdom of the ancients.

However, Wen had something in the very genius of his own understanding that shone out as a light in the ancient gloom that enveloped all about him, even to the lurid mountains, the bright valley, and the cheerful upturned roof of the comfortable, rambling home. Perhaps it was this very gloom, conceived, however, only by himself, that eventually made the fire of his own genius burn more brightly.

Down from the purple mountain of the Plowshare, the terraced paths led out through the gay fields of the Vale of Blue, aglow in the golden sunshine of Kwantung's long-enduring summer;

53

and yet, despite the beauty of the land that was his home, the helpless lad realized that it was enshrouded in a thick veil of ignorance that none had had the courage to rend asunder.

With no friend or companion, no tutor or teacher, no kin of blood or kith of relationship to whom he could confide his doubts and perplexities, the peasant lad of Blue Valley searched his own soul by the light of his own reasoning, and, ever working at the jumble of the classics, comforted himself again and again with the thought: "There is other wisdom, but it must be found beyond Blue Valley. Some day I shall go forth and seek this wisdom, and then this gloom shall not endure."

# VIII

## THE TALE OF THE RIVER PIRATES

WHILE Wen was standing up with his face to the wall of the village temple school, in the ease with which he acquired the classics he found time to do some thinking that was not included in the wisdom of the ancients.

In the school there was no chance to learn anything about a government, for Chinese in the Manchu day were not allowed to teach or talk politics. The few Chinese who violated this law soon had little use for their tongues, for before long their trunkless heads gaped upon the dust of the Manchu execution-ground. Whatever else they were, the Manchus were apt and clever in the use of the executioner's sharp, heavy sword. This sword was the Manchu panacea for all political ills. The Manchus had won the country by the sword, and what else was there for them to do save hold the sword?

Sun Yat Sen as a lad had no opportunity to know about good government, since there was no one about him who knew what government meant

55

other than the threat of the sword or the lance of the Manchu soldier. Early in his father's orderly management of his home, Sun Yat Sen conceived, in the quickness of his natural intelligence, that if a large household such as his father's could be governed from within, each member respecting the rights of the others and accepting the house-governing rules of the head of the household, likewise a government as between such families could be run by respecting and enforcing respect, each family holding to its duty to the others.

Up to the day he left China for the first time, Sun had never had from any source other than his own any observation on the subject of government. One of the first things a school-boy learns in the Occident is the name of the contemporary hero, or the great men of the time. But for the school-boy Sun there was no such teaching. He was taught the wisdom of Confucius and Mencius of some two thousand years gone by, but as to the actual conditions of China he was taught nothing, for no one knew anything of real history in the whole village. There was some talk of the long-haired rebels, but it was a vague story. Hence Wen's independent thinking had only progressed from a comparison of his own home government with the Manchu control.

Then came the great object-lesson of the river pirates.

One day he was at his class at the village school when all was thrown into confusion by the sound of murderous calls and commands, to the accompaniment of a great battering-ram whose swinging blows against walls of stone echoed down through the streets of Choy Hung. It was an attack by the river pirates on the house of a returned emigrant who had made a fortune in America. He had constructed the door of his house with a double beam that made it, as he thought, impregnable even against the attacks of the pirates. But the pirates betook themselves to rigging up a battering-ram with which to attempt to break an opening through the stone wall of the house and thus possess themselves of the considerable fortune that the owner kept therein.

The river pirates of Kwantung are, perhaps, the most bloodthirsty and ingenious of all followers of the black flag. The fierce pirates of the Spanish Main appear as amiable and benevolent as Robin Hoods compared to these rapacious vultures of Kwantung's rivers and valleys.[1] There was a price on the tousled head of every one of them; and on the theory that they might as well

[1] Since Sun Yat Sen has been in control of Kwantung these river pirates are becoming a page of the past.

57

lose their heads for a dozen murders as for one they entered into the game of robbing and killing with a cheerful deviltry and courageous malice that knew no bounds. As a business proposition, a few minutes of bloody work were the alternative they offered in the event of any resistance of their band.

However, the pirates had picked a stubborn and courageous victim when they tackled the rich returned emigrant of Blue Valley. Moreover, this emigrant had confidence in the ability of his walls to withstand the fiercest onslaught; so he cried out his defiance and awaited the attack with that fortitude so common among the Chinese.

But, alas! He had not considered the efficacy of the pirates' battering-ram, which, made from the heavy timbers of their craft, was lightly swung with supple hawsers and manipulated back and forth with an energy that even the piratical confidence in this uneven battle did not slacken.

Boom! Bang! Boom! Bang! The ram swings back and forth, the ponderous blows echoing through the streets of the hamlet.

Boom! Bang! Boom! Bang! And the crash and thud strike terror into the hearts of the villagers of Blue Valley.

Terrified mothers gather up their frightened children to hide them pell-mell as best they can.

The whole school is thrown into consternation at the first alarm, and teachers and scholars scatter in wild confusion in their efforts to seek refuge.

However, as they flee for safety, there is just one who stands bravely forth, a little pigtailed school-boy who, walking out into the open, little by little advances directly and without hesitation to where the pirates are engaged in their wicked onslaught.

There is no sign of fear on his youthful face as he indignantly stands and watches the pirates, who are so busy in their attack that they do not notice the tiny fellow.

Boom! Bang! Boom! Bang! and splinters of oak and fragments of stone are showered upon the brave little head with the braided queue. Cries of terror come from within the walls as the great battering-ram crashes deeper and more heavily into the stone masonry and loosens the beams from their beds of cement. Now the wall is breaking to fragments beneath those final blows, struck with a desperation born from the stubbornness of the resistance. The tiny boy in Nanking blue still stands his ground, fearing neither the ferocity of the pirates nor the flying splinters nor the shower of sharp stones.

Boom! Bang! Crash! and the gate of the wall falls in a cloud of dust, while the pirates, swords in hand, spring into the breach to seek their victim, dashing past the diminutive but undaunted lad.

Ah! Now the pirates are within, and utter cries of rage when they find their proposed victims have escaped by a smaller service-gate in the rear. Then loud and angry outbursts are finally turned into shouts of exultation as the treasure-boxes of the returned emigrant are found and the gold measured up with piratical bursts of boasting.

Then the pirates come out laughing. Now they are joyous and exultant. Ah! Their labor has been well repaid. They have no thoughts of murder now. The plunder is rich; their joy in the possession of the precious loot has overcome the battle-surge of their wickedness. As they go down to the water heavily laden with their spoil, they brush aside the tiny figure that now has a look of scorn and contempt upon its face as though to cry out against the outrage. The pirates sail away. No sooner have they left than a wan, disheveled figure appears upon the broken ruins of the wall, crying out in despair:

"I am ruined! The pirates have taken my all! For long years I risked my life at hard labor in the land of the Ocean-men to gather wealth for the benefit of my family and my townsmen; but now the pirates have taken my all. Ah, that I had remained in the land of the Ocean-men, where there are leaders honest and true! In that land the law gives a man protection, while here in China we have prohibitions but no protection."

With the last exultant chantey call of the pirates echoing up the river, the little bystander, himself destined to become a great leader of good against the forces of evil, reflects:

"Why does not China have laws such as the laws of the Ocean-men? Why should this emigrant, who at the peril of his life amassed honestly his fortune, which the Ocean-men allowed him to bring back with him—why should he not have the protection of the law here in China?"

Up to the time of this tragedy it had appeared quite natural for him to fall in line with the reason of his elders, who declared that the river pirates were as inevitable an evil as the locust pest and the drouth. "Choy Hung," so reasoned the elders, "was near to Kam Shing anchorage, and therefore it was natural that the pirates should come up to loot and pillage Choy Hung. It had been done from time immemorial, and why should it not be done again? Piracy was like the famine or like sickness. It could not be circumvented. The proper way to defeat the pirates was to dispose of the treasure in such wise that the pirates could find nothing. The proverbial beggar was

61

right when he declared at the gate, 'Please give me only one cash, for if you give me more they will rob me of it.' ''

This philosophy, according to the village elders, established a rule safe to follow. If you had but a mite the pirates would not bother you; if you had too much you should find some way of fooling the robbers into believing that you had only a mite. A rare philosophy but perfectly sane under the Manchu dynasty.

However, I know that the brave little boy in blue that went back to the empty school from the gutted and ruined home had in his heart a feeling that in the land of the Ocean-men was some power that could even punish pirates.

He was now resolved more than ever to go overseas and know the Ocean-men's way.

# IX

### THE MANDARINS AND THE RICH BROTHERS

IN THE town of Blue Valley there was a family
of three brothers. They had been poor, but
they had grown rich—and honestly. Opulence
and abundance attended them because of their industry and perseverance. The Chinese do not
envy the rich as do the poor of the Occident, for
the rich in China are only moderately rich and
do not bear heavily upon the poor. At all events,
the Sun family had esteem but not envy for the
family of the three rich brothers. The three had
gained their fortune honestly; why should they
not enjoy it? Some day a member of the Sun
family would become rich; therefore, should the
example of the regard for the rich not be in order?

So the three rich brothers and their families
still remained friends of the Suns. Wealth had
not raised a barrier between them. Little Wen
used to play in the garden of the three rich
brothers. He had great respect for them, for his
father said that their wealth was legitimately

acquired. Little Wen loved the garden. I have spoken of his love for birds, how he wanted to have a singing bird. Sun loves nature, and as a boy that garden was to him a delight. Besides, it was the garden of the three brothers who were the friends of his father, and it is nice to be in the garden of people you like.

Then one day when Wen was playing in this garden there was a great alarm raised, and in a cloud of dust scores of heavily armed Manchu soldiers and yamen runners and Mandarin harpies swooped down upon the garden and upon the homes of the three brothers that were built about it.

Having possessed themselves of the whole compound and surrounded the houses, they brought out the three brothers, loaded them with chains, and marched them off to their doom, while the Mandarins remained in possession of the fortunes and homes of the three unfortunate men. Later on it was known that one of these brothers had had his head struck off like a common river pirate on the execution-grounds of Canton, while the other two languished in prison. In spite of many inquiries, no one in Choy Hung could ascertain upon what charge these men were punished. All Choy Hung was rebellious against this outrage, which every villager knew had as its object the

". . . despite the beauty of the land that was his home, the help-less lad realized that it was enshrouded in a thick veil of igno-rance that none had had the courage to rend asunder" (Page 54).

Of such bridges there are several thousand for every mile of rail-road in China.

Fisherman with his fishing-birds. Even he is awakening to the advantage of railroads, such as preached by Dr. Sun.

despoilment of the three rich brothers. The villagers murmured in indignation among themselves. They did not dare speak openly.

There was, however, one little school-boy in the town of Blue Valley who made up his mind to enter a protest against this injustice, come what might. With his head held high and a brave, undaunted heart, he walked up the hill to the garden of the three brothers. Oh, how changed it was! The fountain and statues in fragments; the trees and flower-beds stripped; everything broken, stolen, or neglected. Wen had come through a broken wall, and as he was gazing about on the scene that was so changed and desolate, a Manchu officer with his dangling sword came up. Little Wen stood his ground.

"What dost thou here?"

"I come to visit the garden of the three brothers. This is their garden. They are friends of my family. I come to enjoy their garden."

"What sayest thou?" declared the officer, hardly controlling himself from rage.

"I say that I have come here to enjoy the garden of my friends, the three brothers. They were always good to me, and this is their garden, and they, too, should be allowed to enjoy it. Why have you taken it from them? Why have you loaded them with chains? Why have you be-

65

headed one of them? Why do you keep the others in prison?"

"What!" cried out the officer, infuriated at the stanch stand the little lad had taken. "I will teach you how to enjoy the garden of your friends, the three brothers"; and he made a savage lunge at the little fellow who, however, nimbly escaped and made his way homeward, delighted with the fact that he, of all the village, had been able to lodge a protest against the injustice perpetrated upon the three brothers.

## X

### THE WHITE DEED

TAX-PAYING has never been a popular pastime, even in our own highly developed state of society. In fact, I think that the Chinese have always paid their taxes with less grumbling than we; for Chinese tax-paying is a family affair, of which the final accomplishment means a new lease of domestic life in its struggle for survival. There are limits even to Chinese forbearance; among these limits is the affliction of tax-paying on the "white deed."

In the Sun family this "white deed" episode finds its origin in the original acquisition of land on the part of the Blue Valley settlers of the Sun family. These settlers had acquired several thousand mow of land (a mow is one-seventh of an acre) and, as time ran along, had sold off a parcel from these holdings as occasion offered or necessity demanded. These sales are always made in accordance with the Chinese custom of a "white deed" transaction; the expense of having a deed "made red" by affixing the official stamps involved such an extortionate expense that the grantors merely gave a formal instrument in the nature of a land contract which acted as an unregistered deed. This makeshift gave possession under an equitable title to the grantee, but left the legal tax-assessing title in the grantor, the grantor still being the owner of record. Hence, although the Sun family had sold off much of the original holdings, on the land registers they still continued to be the record owners, and solely responsible for the payment of the taxes.

Hence, every year, the tax-collector would come around to the head of the Sun family and collect from him the taxes for a substantial part of all the farmers in the Choy Hung neighborhood. The tax-collector knew, of course, that the Suns no longer owned the land, and also knew that the Suns, in their turn, would have to go to the trouble of collecting the taxes from all those who held under the "white deeds."

Every year the collection worked additional hardships on the Sun family, for to "save their faces" and to protect the "white deed," they had to go plodding round to find out who were the actual owners of the land, and then collect the taxes which, in turn, they would (if they were able to collect them) hand over to the tax-collector. At all events, the Suns had to pay the taxes on the whole original acquisition of land.

68

The many parcels of the original property were changing hands continually, and it was indeed hard to keep up with the reparceling of the original tracts, but no matter how great the hardships the head of the Sun family had to pay the taxes.

Bad as the matter was, it suddenly became worse, for the representative head of the Sun family for that period died, and the father of Sun Yat Sen found himself sorely inflicted with the worries and anxieties of the "white deed" tax-collecting. The elder Sun had not anticipated the onerous duties of this burdensome imposition. Several generations had now elapsed since the original grant to the Sun family. Landmarks had been changed, the original markings lost or buried under the plow; and when the tax-collector finally came to the door of Sun Yat Sen's father the condition of the title to the land was so involved that it was difficult to make any satisfactory adjustment among the various landholders. For, as already noted, the original property was all assessed still in the ancient settler of the Sun family, and the different tracts now varied so much in value, because of the various conditions of the improvements, that it would have taken up the entire time of a numerous board of equalization for days to fix on an equitable adjustment of the assessment.

Hence, this obligation descended like a black cloud upon the household of the Suns, even affecting with its depressing influence little Sun Yat Sen himself. It was as if a summons in a continual lawsuit had been served upon the whole family, of which each member participated in a long-drawn-out sorrow which they were to share together for an indefinite if not endless period. There was no relief to be had, except by continued bribing of the tax-collector. The only permanent relief would be through the establishment of a new registry, which would cost a ruinous sum.

So great was the perturbation in the Sun family that it left a lasting impression on the Reformer's mind.

"Again and again I asked myself," Sun confided to me, "why should the Mandarins put such a 'squeeze' upon the 'red deeds' as to exact the makeshift of 'white deeds'? Why did not the Mandarins follow the moral teachings of the classics? Why should the so-called Son of Heaven permit such an unjust condition of the law as to require his subjects to use subterfuges to escape the heavy load of taxation the mandarinate laid upon the people? And again and again I asserted to myself, 'surely there must be some remedy against this wickedness of the Mandarins.' "

Finally the little school lad mustered up his

courage and asked one of the village elders if the injustice could not be remedied. The elder shook his head sadly and answered:

"No, Wen, there is no remedy; for it is the rule of the Son of Heaven."

## XI

### THE LITTLE SEARCHER FOR TRUTH

THE Reformer told me that the most disheart-ening feature of his Choy Hung early life was the absence of any source of information of educative value. His mind was always asking questions which he knew could not find an answer. There was no one in the village who could give him the reason for the questions that rose up to trouble him. He was continually hearing of the wisdom of the ancients, and yet he could not find a reason why this wisdom was wise.

After the three brothers' episode he became much interested in the meaning of authority. Who was it that gave the brutal officer the right to beat others and to load them with chains? Was it because the officer was strong and had weapons, or was it because some one else stronger than he gave him this wanton authority? Who was it that ordered the execution of one of the honest three brothers and held the others in prison?

"What did they say about Peking in those early days, Doctor?"

"Up to my thirteenth year, when I left China

72

for Honolulu, I do not remember ever hearing of
Peking as the center of imperial authority. All
the authority of the village of Choy Hung only
went as far as Heang Shang, which was the district city for our hamlet. Around it the mild, un-
changing life of the villagers moved in a political
and social regularity as of satellites forever fixed
in their orbits. Peking meant nothing to us, for
Choy Hung and the other villages about it considered Heang Shang as the final authority in all
matters of law and order.''

"Did not the villagers of Choy Hung care anything about the higher authority that gave Heang
Shang its right to rule through its mandarins?''

"The villagers of Choy Hung were so disgusted
with its authority that they had just as little to
do as possible with the officials of Heang Shang,
and of course they dared not go any farther than
Heang Shang in anything that concerned authority. The village elders required that all the villagers be prompt in their obligations toward
Heang Shang, since they looked upon the accomplishment of this duty much as they would the
bribing of the river pirates. They paid to be left
alone.''

I gather from what Dr. Sun told me of that
early period that his father would gladly have interested himself in the authority that governed

him had it not been indiscreet to the point of danger to inform himself in such regard. Even as a tiller of the soil, Sun's father knew that it is dangerous business to know too much about government. The Taiping Rebellion was still fresh in his mind, and since the "long-haired rebels" had failed so dismally and paid with their heads for their temerity in inquiring into politics, he, no doubt, with the majority of his generation, believed in a most discreet ignorance in all matters concerning authority.

There was one thing, however, that was impressed upon young Sun's mind from the earliest period of his recollection, that the actual and highest ruler of the great Chinese world was not a Chinese but a foreigner. This declaration, half whispered about, made a deep impression on Wen's mind.

"The ruler of the Chinese is not Chinese? Why?"

He made his mother his confidant in his search for information. She herself did the best she could to help him on his search for the truth, but, alas, she was only a Chinese woman!

Finding that his mother could, as his closest friend, give him no political information, he considered that she might help him out in some of the other problems that were worrying him.

The expression "ten thousand years" is used most frequently as a Chinese superlative. One day the little fellow asked his mother:

"How much time is ten thousand years?"

"It is such a long time that no one knows," responded his mother.

Another time he asked her, "What is the heaven, the blue sky, made of?"

"It is made like a *kwo* turned upside down." A *kwo* is a family rice-dish.

"But are there not other *kwos* over the first one?" asked the lad. The dear old mother could not answer.

His earliest conception of immortality came one day when he asked his mother:

"What happens to persons when they die?"

"All is ended, Wen; death ends all," sadly declared his mother.

"But I don't want my life to end when I am dead," asserted the poor little searcher after the truth. Alas! even his mother had no information from which to draw comfort. She could only give him her love.

I did not bother the Reformer to recall much of the details of the ancestral worship of his home, for, as already stated, the ancestral tombs of the Suns were not at Choy Hung, and the ancestral rites are more commonplace in their observance

75

than many other Chinese customs. He informed me, however, that very early in his childhood he discovered an excellent reason for ancestral worship and considered it a most meritorious act. It was right to obey one's father and mother, for they were the creators of the child's being, and in honoring them honor should, likewise, be paid to the fathers and mothers of each known generation.

## XII

### WEN'S FIRST ATTEMPT AT REFORM

IT IS hard to understand how Wen, the little Chinese boy, out of his own nature alone, with nothing to help him from his surroundings, began to perceive that many of the things going on about him were wrong. Unlike the mass of Chinese, in his mind there was a God-given instinct that taught that not all of the old Chinese customs were good.

Now, foot-binding was from the Chinese viewpoint a good Chinese custom which all the members of the family indorsed with zest, for it maintained the respect of the family by showing that they conformed to custom. The victim endured stoically the years of torture, sustained by the thought that eventually she would wear the badge of a highly respectable Chinese lady.

The original idea of foot-binding presumably started in the imperial harem, where the girl victims had special treatment, including elevation of the feet and the administration of opium, both to relieve them from pains as well as to hold the foot to something of its original shape; for a great percentage of these foot-bindings result in mutilation that makes the existence of the victim that of a lifetime invalid. Many die of blood-poison, and I recall a young beggar woman who used to drag herself around on her knees in the vicinity of Quinsan Gardens in Shanghai, who had had one foot rotted off by the process, but who, as she went around on her knees begging, would hold the remaining tiny foot up very proudly, to show that she had, at all events, something of the quality of a Chinese lady.

However, sometimes special and expert service in the binding of a girl's feet results in very small baby feet in the grown woman, which do not entirely detract from grace in walking; for the light toddling and tumbling forward with each step gives a graceful poise to the body, which has a great charm to the Chinese; indeed, this peculiar totter in the carriage gives the victim herself a great self-confidence through the addition to her beauty.

Attempts at foot-binding among the masses, with no precautions, result in great malpractices and in loss of limb and even life itself. Instead of frequent changes of the bands of cloth, the old bandages, soiled and filled with pus, are allowed to remain until they start complications that eventually club the foot, and nearly always break the arches, leaving a hoof-like deformity which makes the victim a hopeless cripple for life. Even the great percentage of cases of "successful" foot-binding results not only in a most distressing deformity to the feet, but in injury to the ankles as well; and as to the toes; well, the toes club up under the feet, making walking, even on the balls of the feet, excruciatingly painful.

The Sun family, being intensely Chinese, believed in all Chinese customs, including even foot-binding. Sun Yat Sen's mother had come out of the foot-binding terror with great good luck for, as will be seen from the picture shown herewith, her feet had been bound so successfully and had become so small that she was obliged to carry a staff to sustain her as the years rolled along. It seems to me, however, that I can note from a study of this dear Chinese mother that there is still shown on her face something of the suffering which she endured in having her feet bound.

The Suns, in their hearts, undoubtedly admitted something of the barbarity of the practice, but it was Chinese, and therefore good; so Sun Yat Sen's sister came up for her share of the foot-binding agony. Stoically she submitted to the clamp of the bandages which hold the foot riveted in an iron-like grasp, destroying the circulation of the blood in the lower limbs and setting the whole nervous system in mad rebellion against the torture. Night after night she would toss, moan, and murmur in her attempt to endure the pain, stoically awaiting for the dawn to come when she might have some rude treatment in an attempt to alleviate the pain. But with the dawn, her system racked with fatigue and pain, her sad lamentations would commence anew.

Finally Wen could stand it no longer. He loved his sister just as he loved every other member of the family circle. He went bravely to his mother.

"Oh, Mother, the pain is too great for her! Please do not bind the feet of my sister."

It was one of Sun's first pleas for reform. His mother shook her head sadly. I presume that she was somewhat shocked at this insubordination on the part of the good little brother Wen. I suppose that it seemed to her that Wen was disloyal to his sister in not wanting her to have pretty little feet.

"Wen, how can your sister have lily-like feet if she does not endure the pain? And, after all, it may not last so very long. Your sister is having good treatment. She is getting along very nicely. Your sister will be sorry when she grows up and reproach us if we neglect to give her the benefit

80

This newer home "was built by Sun Yat Sen's mother with money given her by Da Ko, of whom we shall hear much as we go along" (Page 39).

The new modern town school at Blue Valley, very different from the village Temple School where Wen went to shout, "Out with the rest the senseless repetition of the three-syllable classic" (Page 51).

Earliest picture of Sun Yat Sen, taken when he was about eighteen. His skullcap hides his queue.

Letter to the author from Mrs. Sun which accompanied the earliest picture of Dr. Sun.

of the foot-binding in conformity with the good Chinese custom."

Wen earnestly listened to the sentiment of his mother expressed in words to the above effect. Again, however, he renewed his protests, declaring that there was no reason why Chinese women should mutilate their feet. Whereupon his mother brought forth the new and forceful argument of referring to the Hakkas. The Hakkas were an alien people who lived in that part of Kwantung. The Chinese did not consider the Hakkas their equal.

"Behold the Hakkas!" declared the mother of Wen. "No Hakka woman has bound feet. The Hakkas do not bind their feet as do the Bandis or Chinese. Would you have your sister a Hakka woman or a Chinese woman? Would you have her as a stranger or as one of us?"

This, however, did not settle the argument nor end the protest. Finally, the mother, with her love for her son, and with her pity awakened anew for her daughter, became so affected that she refused to bind her daughter's feet any longer and, Chinese fashion, turned the hard-hearted job over to a woman specialist of the village, who, in spite of Wen's continued protests, prosecuted the practice to a successful end.

Sun, through his political influence, has done

much to abolish this practice, which, fortunately, is now passing away.

I have indulged in the over-lengthy discussion of this episode because it seemed to me important in portraying the early character of the great Reformer, whose first reform was commenced at his own home-side in the plea, "Please do not bind my sister's feet."

## XIII

### MEN IN SHACKLES

AS HE grew older, again and again in his search for truth young Wen waked up the village elders of the hamlet of Blue Valley. With that good-natured indulgence that Chinese elders assume toward the weaknesses of childhood, they had heard of his protests against the binding of the feet of his sister. As long as he confined his reform "mischief" to the family circle it was all right; but the village elders were not prepared to allow any youthful admonitions to disturb the tranquil lethargy of their hidebound village control. Eventually, however, not only in the family circle did Wen utter protests against the ignorance and superstition that were going about him like a wheel of fate, and which he felt instinctively to be wrong, but even in the presence of the village elders he would make observations which shocked the old fellows beyond measure.

For example, in Choy Hung there were three Chinese families who owned slaves; not really slaves in the sense of the former African slaves of America, slaves that could be bought and sold, but still slaves as far as a dependent's full freedom went.

These slaves were acquired originally by a parent's selling a son into bondage. This practice, which still prevails in China, is something akin to the old English indenture system of binding out a boy or a girl, but it is much more severe. Girls sold into bondage could acquire their freedom from this modified form of slavery by marriage. The boys grew up under varying degrees of restraint, and the master had the right even to flog his bondman for a misdemeanor, although the flogging had to be done in public and in the premises of an open temple.

Wen protested vigorously against this system. It was not in accordance with the teachings of the classics. No man had a right to enslave another, even for the time being. Were not the children of these slaves also born into a sort of bondage?

What right had a parent to bind his offspring? Even if this bondage, as among the descendants of the original bondman, became more lax as the years rolled along, it was still a bondage of that man's right to full freedom. It was a restraint prohibited by the classics. And suppose that finally nothing more were left of this bondage than the duty to participate in the prostrations of the family ancestral rights; what right had one man to demand of another a service with no compensation on the other side? How could such prostrations be of any use when they were involuntary?

As he preached against this slavery, Wen showed that even the village elders were slaves themselves; slaves to an iniquitous system of government that made even the village elders bondmen.

However, with all his audacious preachments, Wen realized that he was on dangerous ground, for he had no knowledge of what should be substituted for these absurd old customs. The Manchus were rotten in their government, but if they were overthrown, what would take their place? He could preach reform, but he could propose no method to make such a reform, because he was utterly ignorant of what was going on in more enlightened lands. He had never talked to an actual Ocean-man and knew nothing whatsoever of those lands from which the Ocean-men came. In fact, the Ocean-man did not always enter into his reflections on reform. He found himself face to face with the little body politic of Blue Valley, realizing that the method of reform must come from among the Chinese themselves. Since Manchu rule was wrong, the Chinese must find some better way of attending to the business of the people.

It seemed to him eventually that there was too little government; that the Manchu rule did not try to concern itself with the welfare of the people, merely using its power to extort money from the Chinese and giving them nothing in return; that the authority that the Manchu Government did possess was so weak, wicked, and profligate that within it there was no prospect of reform; that in default of the Government the Chinese tried to find some order in absurd customs to which they clung, since nothing else was offered them.

Sun, even in his childhood, conceived that the Chinese masses were not to blame for following the old customs of child-selling, infanticide, concubinage, foot-binding, idol-worship, and other reprehensible practices. Chinese men, women, and even children were in bondage to custom, and there was no leadership to bring them up from out of the wilderness of custom. Little Wen never dreamt that he himself would become a leader. He merely bethought himself of seeking out some one who would lead him; and in trying to find the leader Sun became a leader himself.

Kipling's Kim had his Lama to follow in his search for the River of Life, but no traveling

priests of the true path came the Blue Valley way.
There was no leader for young Wen to emulate,
no instructor to guide this willing disciple. At
length he came to a psychological change that
brought out protest after protest, audaciously
voiced, to the consternation of the village elders
and even of the family circle.

"Why do we remain in bondage to these
practices?"

And the answer would come:

"These things are right, because they have
always been. The Son of Heaven is our leader,
and these things are lawful to him."

So Wen within his own soul commenced to hate
the Son of Heaven.

If he could find no leader, how could he find the
true way? Alas! the precocious young philosopher
could conceive of no method to get to that path
that led upward.

## XIV

### "CHINA IS THE WORLD"

ONE would imagine there was much that Wen
had to forget of his Chinese teachings in
order even to surmise that there were better
ways; but it was not so.  His young mind clung
tenaciously to whatever it considered good in the
Chinese scheme of personal and social welfare,
while at the same time it absorbed new strength
from the younger virility of his own reflections.
All was not bad in China; much was good, very
good.

But he knew that at least something of the old
had to be put off in order to take on the new; and
even in the immaturity of his youth he early found
that if he should have to go beyond China to find
the new advantages of some clearer life, he would
have to rid himself of those ancient notions of
China which were founded upon the inherited ignorance of centuries.  But this clearer life, where
could it be found?  Why give up the old, not
knowing anything of the new?  He had been
taught that China was a great world sufficient
unto itself.  He now knew that this was false.

China was not the world that he had been led from his babyhood to believe it to be. Along with this idea, he found that if he was to learn the new order of life (whose necessity was now so clearly apparent) he must forget much else of the conceit of that ancient Chinese civilization that had at last stagnated in the surfeit of its racial increase.

Geography in his day was never taught in Chinese schools. The aim of the Manchu dynasty was to keep the people in ignorance even in regard to the extent of China, itself. The Manchu merely taught that the Son of Heaven ruled China and that China was the world. Therefore, the Son of Heaven ruled the world.

Wen had never even heard of a map until one day a school comrade, who had chanced to go over the mountain to a distant town, returned to Blue Valley and breathlessly confided to Wen:

"The priests have a wonderful thing hanging up on the wall of the Temple over there. It answers any questions about mountains, rivers, or cities, even before you ask the question. It tells the traveler the safest way to travel. It shows how far the river-source is from the sea, and how long it takes to go from one city to another."

"What do they call this wonderful thing?" asked Wen.

89

"I don't know what they call it," answered his boy informant.

Wen immediately formed a deep longing to go over to the distant town and visit this wonderful thing that hung on the wall of the Temple. But, alas! he was never able to realize this longing, and it was only when he came to Honolulu that he finally gratified his great curiosity by gazing upon a map.

The information that his school comrade had given him concerning the temple map greatly excited his desire to enter into the mysteries of geography and history and government. How wonderful it would be to live in a town where there was a map hanging on the walls of a temple!

Perhaps there were schools in the land of the Ocean-men, where there were many maps and many other things to teach a reason and to tell how to think and to do. Perhaps this reason was the cause of all the abundance and comfort the emigrants sought overseas. The foreigners perhaps used reason in everything they thought or did; and perchance, above all, their government was filled with wisdom. Perhaps therein was a clearer life. Why should the little village of Choy Hung be in constant fear of river pirates? Why should the Chinese fear to grow rich lest they be despoiled by the tortures of the mandarins? Why should a whole family be thrown into unending trouble because the Government exacted a kind of deed when the people could not pay the tax exacted upon it?

Of course all these inquiries did not force themselves upon the lad's mind in one revelation. He was wonderfully precocious, but at that his mind was undeveloped. However, little by little even his young years gave him to understand that the land of his birth was not the world. China sank in his estimation, not into insignificance, but down to a place of temporary ingloriousness, in the new estimate which he was putting upon things.

Even with Wen's psychological change, China, if not the world, was the land he loved. Above all, he loved the people in the little village of Blue Valley. It was for them that he wanted to find that "clearer life"; and now, only thirteen years of age, he realized that the "clearer life" lay far beyond the waters of Kam Shing, the anchorage of Venus, the Golden Star.

But it lay so far away, that land of the "clearer life"; would he ever be able to reach that shore? China was not the world, for, indeed, there must be something that lay beyond it.

## XV

### DA KO

WE NOW come to a wonderful period in the life of the leader, a period when his hope to see the promised land of the Ocean-men seemed about to be realized, for his brother Da Ko, fifteen years older, had succeeded in overcoming the objections of the family and had gone forth to a midway land; not to the California land of gold and perils, but to a wonderful half-way point, a small country made up of islands and inhabited not so much by white men as by brown natives. There was a city there, and they called it Hon-o-lu-lu.

Yes, surely, now that Da Ko had gone forth, he, Wen, would be able eventually to follow, for it was not so far as the greater land, the California land of gold where one of the family had perished, and the sea not so wide as where the other had gone down.

Hon-o-lu-lu! At first it had been just a name to Wen; a name, a word like any of those words and ideographs that the teacher in the village school was making them sing eternally to fasten them in their memories. Hon-o-lu-lu; now this intimate word of the family circle was taking on a new meaning, a meaning that no other name possessed. It meant a land of promise, a country of better things. It was a good land, for men risked their lives to go there. And it was a better land than China, or else the Chinese would not want to leave China to go to it.

Hon-o-lu-lu! It became the lad's dream. No river pirates and battering-rams, no tax burdens on the poor, no "white deeds," no despoilment of the rich. Yes, that was the reason why men took their lives in their hands to seek out that far-away land of safety and abundance. Ah, if it were possible to go! There were the waters of the Kam Shing anchorage shining anew with every break of dawn; it was so easy to follow the light of the rising sun. Why should n't his dream come true? His brother had gone forth; why could he not follow? Of course his father knew best; but his father had never been in that land of promise.

Da Ko had not been gone a year before they had good news from him. He had arrived in Honolulu safely and was doing well. He told about the beauty of the country, the richness of the soil, the abundance of food, the palm-girt beaches, the orchards and the vineyards—yea, verily, isles of treasure. How eagerly the whole family listened to the reading of the letter, Wen holding his breath from suspense at every word of the news! It would be a long time before another letter came, for there was no Chinese postal service then, and the only way that a letter could be sent and delivered was to wait until an emigrant was coming or going to serve as a personal bearer of the message. They had to wait nearly a year before they could find an emigrant in the district of Kam Shing who was going to Honolulu, and who agreed to carry the answer for them back to Da Ko, the faithful son and brother in the far-away land of bounty. Ah, great was the rejoicing in the Sun family when the returning emigrant was found! At last they could answer Da Ko's message.

How carefully the letter was indited! The Chinese language with its ideographs does not lend itself as easily to the familiarities of family correspondence as do alphabetic tongues. There is a remote sequence in the connection of the ideographs that does not bring home the commonplace emotions of fireside separations as clearly as in the agglutinate languages. Be that as it may, the elder Sun, with his heart fired with ambition for his son, spared no pains in making the

94

message the best product that the combined skill of the whole literary genius of the entire village could summon.

Ah, it was wonderful to think that Da Ko, the elder son, was safe in that far-distant land of perils. The gods had at last been good; and the toll of death, which the two uncles had paid in their supreme efforts to reach that land of plenty, was not to be increased. Long were the admonitions, very touching the greetings, with quotations from the wisdom of the precious classics. At last the Sun family had surmounted the dangers of that perilous land of the West.

But with it the elder Sun was not yet content.

"What folly to wander from the paths of the ancestors!" he declared. "What does it profit a man to gain a hill of gold if he has not the respect of his village? By wandering away one loses this respect."

It was in this conflicting environment, whose sentiments would one day rejoice in the prosperous reports from abroad, and another day lament the departure from the customs of the ancients, that Wen waxed in the wisdom of his dream. Again his dream seemed more real. Again it seemed easier to go. Still, there was great doubt as to the home-coming of Da Ko, the elder brother. To go forth was one thing; to return was another.

95

The winds that took the ship out might not bring it home.

Da Ko in far-off Honolulu prospereu. He was not gifted with the genius of his younger brother, but both had the same resolute qualities of perseverance, observance of proprieties, and endurance. Da Ko succeeded from the start. Where the proud precincts of Pearl Harbor now stand, he started out as the first pioneer in reclaiming swamp-lands on the surf-broken shore. With the sole labor of his two hands, day by day he turned the reedy swamp into a rice-paddy that produced a hundredfold. The hard lessons in land-drainage and soil-culture that he had learned in the faraway fields of the Blue Valley now stood him in good stead. The good-natured Kanakas looked on and wondered and knew that they, too, would share in the bounty of this Chinese intelligence, for food would be more plentiful with the coming of the Chinese harvests. The elder brother not only prospered but with his prosperity gained the respect of the whole community in which he lived.

Such, finally, was the esteem in which he and eventually his Chinese colaborers were held that the people of Hawaii, through their king, invited them to bring other Chinese to continue the wonder of the work, and in order to encourage their emigration offered to pay the set sum of one hun-

Before Sun's revolutions these walls were the undisputed ease-
ment of the Son of Heaven.

Another view of a Peking tower, which sheltered the Son of
Heaven. "So Wen within his own soul began to hate the Son
of Heaven" (Page 87).

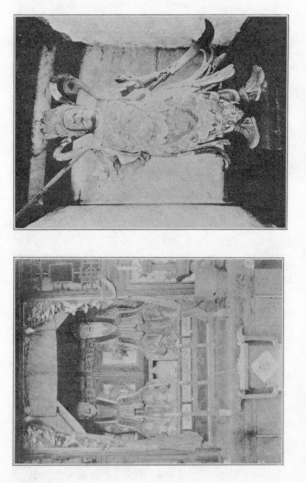

Idols similar to the one mutilated by Wen. "He felt that the Chinese people wanted to go forward but that they would never progress as long as they pinned their spiritual confidence on joss paper and painted gods" (Page 159).

dred dollars for every Chinese that was landed in Hawaii.

While this miracle was being worked in favor of the Sun family in Honolulu, Wen was scoring off the months of his early youth with little variation in the program of his daily school-work and farm toil.

But it was all easier now. Something told him that he was going to the Land of the Clearer Life. With this thought of the "clearer life" the clouded life of the ancients took on a clearer meaning.

He understood and loved the classics now. No more reproofs from his teacher. No more rebellious arguments against the worth of the classics. The incentive of the hoped-for voyage made all learning easy and desirable to him. It was in these early years that Sun Yat Sen laid the foundation of that rare Chinese scholarship which later was to distinguish him in his leadership.

And Wen, likewise, although a lad of a mere dozen years, was beginning to go down into the mysterious depths of Chinese philosophy. It was like going down into a well at high noon, but the deeper he went the clearer shone the blue of the sky above. His teacher now marveled at his progress, for Wen at length realized that if he was to go out to seek that "clearer life" he must take

97

knowledge with him; that no man could find wisdom unless he took knowledge as a compass to find that greater knowledge that lay beyond.

The harder he worked the deeper grew his love for the Chinese classics. At last, in the wisdom of old, there was showing something of the "clearer life"; but it was the rich opaque color of the jade, rather than the transparent beauty of the running brook, so crystalline that all the pebbles showed clear at the bottom. But it was knowledge. It has been the safe chart and guide of China for thousands of years.

It took the time of twelve phasings of the moon to give and receive word from Da Ko. Well, before the next message went back to the elder brother, Wen would have learned all that his village school could give him of the wisdom of the ancients. He made up his mind to be a scholar so that he would know the clearer life when he found it. He struck his mind like a lance into the burnishing depth of Chinese wisdom, and it came forth gilded with the subdued light of the classics. Yes, in the rude temple school of the Blue Valley he planted deep the philosophy of that old wisdom that one day was to grow up into a Tree of Knowledge that grew by the wondrous River of the Clearer Life.

# XVI

## DA KO'S RETURN FROM HONOLULU

TIME rolled along and then the great event happened for which the whole Sun family had so long and tenderly waited. Da Ko, the wanderer, came back.

Three of the Sun family had gone forth to the land of the Ocean-men; Da Ko alone returned. Ah, it was a wonderful home-coming with feasting and merrymaking; for the elder brother had come, and even the widows of the vanished men confessed that he had come from a land of wonders. Da Ko had gone forth as a poor peasant lad and come home rich; not only was he rich in gold but rich in the experience of business well gathered into the storehouse of his brain, and there guarded like a treasure more precious than gold. For this experience showed him how to do things in the Ocean-men's way. Da Ko had conceived and perfected the idea of a partnership that was to take over a large ocean-going ship. In that ship he was to take back to Honolulu Chinese emigrants free of charge, obtaining his reward from the bounty of one hundred dollars

99

per head paid by the king of Hawaii. This amount allowed him a substantial profit over the passage expense of the emigrants.

Da Ko told the wide-eyed wondering group of his possessions in that beautiful island land of the mid-Pacific; told tales of a wondrous beach with sands as yellow as gold and with waters colored like indigo, of a surf that never ceased to break, and of crystal springs that never ran dry. He told of the purple mountains beetling out into the warm sea, sheltering fertile valleys that were bursting in a harvest of fruit and grain, a veritable cornucopia of bounty that never ended in the flow of its treasure.

He told of his own successful work in reclaiming the sea-marshes about Pearl Harbor and bespoke an abundance for every emigrant who would undertake the labor. He declared that the bounty of the land was such that the bronze-skinned natives followed the delights of sea-swimming and garland (lei) stringing rather than hard labor, with no need to worry about food for the morrow. He told of fragrant flowers and singing birds and vales filled with palm and citrus groves and terraces of pineapples.

Was it any wonder that the younger brother was now filled with a burning passion to follow Da Ko back to that land of enchantment? Ah, there he would have a singing bird at last! How his young heart beat with the suspense of the situation!

After a brief visit to Choy Hung, Da Ko prepared to return to take care of the business in Honolulu, leaving the partner he had taken in China to conduct the Chinese branch of the emigrant business which the elder brother had established in the region beyond the Blue Valley.

Wen pleaded with his parents to allow him to return with his elder brother. Oh, how he yearned to go with him! But the stern command of his parents kept Wen at home. One son was enough to risk in the venture.

"Wen, have you forgotten that I lost two brothers over there?" would admonish his father.

Yes, one was enough to risk now in the venture. Perhaps the gods would not be so propitious on the next voyage. The Northern Emperor (the chief village idol) had lost two of his worshipers in the dead brothers who had sailed away to return no more. No, Wen must stay at home.

So the elder brother sailed away and left Wen crushed with disappointment in that humdrum Blue Valley. Time ran along, and at last Da Ko's partner obtained the English steamship *Grannoch,* which had been put under the copartnership management, and the emigrant excursion was finally assembled. The *Grannoch* was to sail from the harbor of Macao. Wen renewed his campaign to go with the ship; he declared that he was no longer a child, that he was in his fourteenth year; why should not he, also, go out to seek his fortune? He would be with friends on the voyage, and his brother would be there at Honolulu to greet him. He had learned all that the temple school could teach him; now there were other schools and other labor that awaited him overseas.

After long implorations and the shrewdest reasoning he could summon to his aid, he finally obtained his parents' consent. Joy! At last his opportunity had come.

Now at last he would know what lay in the world beyond the Blue Valley and the purple mountains of the Plowshare. Yes, all that world that lay beyond Kam Shing, the anchorage of the Golden Star; yes, all that he would know. That new land where there were law, order, and abundance, where there were no pirates, no murderous mandarins, and no "white deeds."

Yes, at last his chance had come. He had no god to thank, and his prayers of gratitude were alone to his parents, for he already hated the good old Northern Emperor idol as much as he hated the Son of Heaven.

But he did feel when the last farewells were

102

said that some divine power greater than any known to the Chinese classicist had entered into his life and granted him an opportunity to go forth and show his worth (if he could prove it!) among those fellow-emigrants in the land where men saw clear.

## XVII

FROM the town of the Blue Valley, Sun Yat Sen, in 1879, then in his fourteenth year, went directly by water to Macao, where the S.S. *Grannoch,* an English iron steamer of some two thousand tons, had been chartered by the partnership of his brother to make the voyage to Honolulu with the Chinese emigrants.

This was the first time that Wen had ever been away from his family. For his thirteen years, he knew, in one way, about as little of what makes up western life as did other Chinese boys at that age. He knew no history except as relating vaguely to Chinese emperors and philosophers, the history that he obtained from the classics. In mathematics he could use the abacus with skill, but of course he had no idea of mental arithmetic, his small idea of mathematics being purely of a mechanical counting-machine kind, and very elementary at that. Of geography, he knew nothing at all, never even having seen a map, although, as we have noted, a school comrade had told him of the map which hung on the temple wall of a dis-

104

tant village. He was well advanced, however, in the ideographs, showing, even at that early age, his scholarly ability in the Chinese written language and forecasting that graceful literary style that distinguishes his high Chinese scholarship to-day. This precocious ability to write a good Chinese style, and likewise his precocious knowledge of the classics, constituted, therefore, about his whole educational stock in trade. He had read nothing except the classics. He had had absolutely no religious training and had never heard of Christ nor of the Jesus men (as the missionaries are called in China), there being no missionaries in the region of the Blue Valley.

But scant as was his education in one way, the thirteen-year-old lad, through reflection, had obtained a wisdom that only the mind of a genius could develop. In the first place he had a clear idea of morality. He had read in the classics:

> The palace a wild for lust;
> The country a wild for hunting;
> Rich wine, seductive music,
> Lofty roofs, carved walls;
> Given any one of these
> And the result can only be ruin.

Such lines, as a rule, mean little to the impulsive lad of thirteen, but when Sun Yat Sen came to Macao, that brilliant city with the lurid gaming-halls, the opium resorts, the flower-boats, and the

105

singsong girl allurements, he knew that all that was wrong; not wrong because it was contrary to religious teaching (for he had none of that), but because it brought disappointment in the end and did injury to the other members of the family circle. The prodigal display of dissipation was so against his nature that he did not even have the boyish curiosity to inquire further into it. He did not even go ashore.

"What impressed you most when you got on that iron ship?" I asked. He leaned back in his chair and studied deeply.

"Oh, there was so much!" he exclaimed. "But I think more than the wonder of the engine, and more than the wonder of the flaming boilers, was just a beam of iron that reached through one side of the ship to the other, to strengthen it. To me it appeared to be a most colossal affair, and I remember wondering how, with its great weight, enough men could get hold of it to put it into its place. This thought flashed through my mind, that the same mechanical genius that had made the great iron girder had also devised means to handle it mechanically. I immediately realized that something was wrong with China, for we could not do the things that the foreigners do. If the foreigners could make and raise into place those massive girders of solid metal, was it not an

106

indication that they were superior to us in other respects?''

Yes, it was a lesson. That iron girder had preached for Wen an eloquent sermon. Here was a young master-mind seeking the truth, and even the commonplace girders of the ship did not escape his attention. He found his sermon in iron just as the exiled duke in Shakespeare's ''As You Like It'' found his sermon in stones and running brooks.

Sun Yat Sen is frequently accused of being anti-foreign. The boy Wen had the same character and impulses as Sun Yat Sen, the President of the Republic of China. The Chinese child is, especially, ever Father to the man. Had Wen gone on that ship with the usual hostile feeling that many Chinese have against the foreigner, he would never have found a sermon in the beam of steel. That his mind was even at that time great enough to make truthful comparisons unfavorable to the land he loved, shows an ingenuousness and receptivity that is remarkable to one knowing the usual cast-iron mold of the Chinese mind. The iron beam was to him emblematic of the New World, just as the battering-ram of the river pirates was emblematic of the Old.

## XVIII

WITH us, a conscience implies some religious background. But here we have a thirteen-year-old boy making what, to him, is a voyage of perils, who knows not God, nor biblical hell nor heaven, and who has been taught by a good mother that death ends all, but who, still, has a conscience and a deeper and more colorful background to that conscience than many who have had larger religious advantages.

And this conscience, From what did it form itself? Not from the sheer literary ideas and generalities of philosophy that he had learned from the pedantic teacher in the temple school? Not from the most difficult constructions of which the Chinese language is capable, and which he had been compelled to learn from the very first year he was at school? No, not from these, but from the natural logic of his own reason; and thanks to this sense of reason, even at the tender age when he first went to the Blue Valley school, I believe that if anybody had read him the Sermon on the Mount he would have understood it.

The S.S. *Grannoch,* as an English ship, was manned by English sailors. One of the sailors died on the journey. His body was hardly cold before it was sewed up in a coarse canvas and laid out upon the deck, weighted with iron. Wen spoke no English and knew little of the meaning of what was going on in the disposition of the remains, except as he reasoned it out himself.

The canvas containing the corpse was slid over the side of the ship where there was an opening to the sea. A bright-colored flag was placed about it, a bell was tolled, the captain of the ship read something from a book, and with a flash and a splash, over went the corpse into the sea.

Wen's mind rebelled at this apparently wanton exhibition of disrespect to the dead. What right had the captain to drop the body (which, although lifeless, did not belong to him) over into the deep ocean? The remains belonged to the dead sailor's family. As a matter of property right, the corpse should have been returned to the family, so that the ceremonies of *feng sui*—the doctrine of the wind and waters—could be properly and decorously performed. From Wen's Chinese teaching, such trifling with the mystery of death was barbarous.

He knew nothing of what the ship's captain was reading from the book, for he did not understand

109

that there was such a thing as prayer. Even had he understood the meaning of the words of the prayer that was read, it would have had no real significance for him, for a Christian prayer had naught in its understanding common to the teaching of the Blue Valley school.

But the seeming barbarity of the burial, the sacrilege of plunging the body of the dead into the unfathomed water to become a prey to the monsters of the deep—how atrocious! With the shock came the realization that he was going to a land whose morals in themselves were different from those of China; whether for better or for worse, he could not imagine. After all, the burial occurred at sea, and perhaps the Ocean-men did not behave so badly on land; perhaps the barbarous burial was an exception and the captain was a brute.

With this object-lesson of the sea-burial he started a new train of reflections. He realized that his Chinese mold of thought was being fused into a new form by the very force of the strange influences that were now beginning to flow into it. He must be careful to have the mold of his thought formed right. Now he would not judge. He had been brought up to believe that China was the universe, that her laws and ways were the acme of wisdom. Now he saw and felt clearly

110

that there were other ways, and that they were not those of the "China World."

The sermon in the beam of iron was clearer to him than the lesson from the burial at sea. Surely the men who had the genius to make and direct a ship of iron were not bad men, for they had no reason to be. But the burial at sea—well, he would know better when he had come to the Land of Bounty.

# SECOND PERIOD

## 1879 to 1883, and Part of 1886
### AMERICAN INFLUENCE—TWO SOJOURNS IN HONOLULU

## XIX

### HONOLULU

A LTHOUGH the journey to Honolulu was attended with comfort, poignant homesickness beset the youth. Indeed, earnestly did he yearn at times to be back in the dear yet simple surroundings of Blue Valley.

He realized now as never before the contentment and happiness of family life, the pleasure of even commonplace greetings among the members of the family circle, and the confidences that grew up in the communal struggle for the good of the household; all these now took on a sweeter meaning. Oh, how hard he would work for the good of that household!

The ship was filled with Chinese emigrants, but he found no close friend among them, and almost in solitude the twenty-odd days of the southerly and pleasant voyage were passed in general observation and reflection. He regretted that from the midst of the very ship that was taking him to the Land of the Clearer Life he could obtain but little information concerning what it was.

And then they came to Honolulu. It seemed

great and wonderful to him, although at that time (1879) it was a very much smaller place than now. The king's large palace was not built then, but the old post-office—now long since gone—with its verandas and railings, seemed very wonderful.

"The old Honolulu post-office still stands out in my mind very clearly," said Sun Yat Sen. "I looked upon it as a wonder-house, for they told me that by merely stamping and addressing a letter and dropping it into a box I could send it back to China as speedily as a ship could go, without having to wait for weeks and even months to find some emigrant to act as a personal messenger."

Above all, Wen was impressed by the orderliness of conditions about him. Everywhere he saw evidences of respect for the law and a confidence in its protection. He noted that the Kanakas (the original inhabitants of the islands) had evidently given up the actual control of the government to Americans, although there was a Kanaka as nominal king on the native throne. He did not wonder at the amiability of the racial conditions existing in Hawaii, for his Chinese nature had that broad perspective in regard to races that may well serve as a model to certain other peoples.

He was not surprised to find that the Americans were controlling a country which, in fact, had been long the inheritance of another people. He saw that it was for the good of the Kanakas, and that they were satisfied with the conditions of the people.

And why? Because there was law, just the sort of law that the Choy Hung victim of the river pirates had declared did not exist in China. Here there were no river pirates with their battering-rams and jingal blunderbusses,[1] no mandarinate marauders, no "white deed" tax-collectors. He might have recalled the old Chinese maxim, "While ye live, enter not a Yamen: when ye die, descend not to hell." He rejoiced when he found that there were no yamens [2] in this new land of abundance.

So great was the prosperity, the ease, the comfort, the abundance of everything about him, he could not but trace their cause to that mysterious thing called Law, which was good in Hawaii because there were no Manchu yamens about.

He realized that Honolulu was under the influences of great and strong forces, and that the law-abiding progress of the Hawaiian Islands came from the motives of that new American civilization, whose life was pulsing out over the waters of the Pacific. America became a dear

[1] The jingal was the old Chinese firearm fired by one man while another held it.
[2] Yamen: the headquarters of a mandarin's authority.

117

name to him. He began to learn some of its songs and know something of its history. He soon looked upon it as verily "the land of the free and the home of the brave," and his reflections led him to believe that it was the American sort of law that China so sorely needed.

He put forth every effort to acquaint himself with the new scheme of education that was offered him. Although on the ship he had known something of what Sunday was for the first time in his life, it was only at Honolulu that he learned the real value of the day of rest. Ordinarily, in China, only the more heavily worked crafts take days of rest, and they limit these days usually to not more than two a month, one at the new and one at the full moon, thus having something of an irregular, unfixed day of repose every fortnight. This rule, however, was only casually observed.

The Christian observance of the Sabbath with its strange church ceremonies was thus at first a puzzle to him. He took it to be a part of the whole program of the Law. As has already been observed, he had had no religious teaching. In Blue Valley he had never taken any save a contemptuous interest in the painted gods of the village temple. From his earliest recollections he had nothing but animadversion for the Northern Emperor and his two consorts (the three village

118

idols), a state of mind manifested dramatically in the sacrilege of which I shall speak later in the chapter on "The Painted Gods of Choy Hung."

In the midst of this new, calm environment of the Ocean-men, the romance of some inexplicable ambition stirred his young mind. He was not conscious of any ambition, for it was a part of his genius and, moreover, was impersonal. By this I mean that even in this early period of his life Sun Yat Sen had subconsciously merged his own self into a plan. He did not know what the plan was, but he already felt that it was something far greater than his own life. Later on, he was to find that the whole purpose of his existence was to be devoted to the accomplishment of this plan —this plan which was greater than self.

Ask the democratic Chinese the reasons for Sun's acknowledged leadership, and perhaps he will say, "Because of his personality and his principles"; but the closer and added reason, it would seem, is that Sun is impersonal in his ambition.

In all my intimate acquaintance with the Great Leader, I have never noticed the slightest indication of egotism. It is not for himself he thinks, but ever of that welfare of the Chinese race for which he is constantly struggling.

In those Honolulu days of his youth, he did not realize that he was a keen observer. He was not old enough to put an estimate upon himself. He came to the new land with no false notions. He had no hatreds, no animosities. His mind was open and receptive to all influences whether good or bad. His young manhood, just emerging from a precocious childhood, was calm and serene. Even his immaturity allowed him reflections upon China, as he compared it with the new land into which he had come. Had he never had the good fortune to go to Hawaii, perhaps he would never have known any other influence save that of China. But, still, he would have been a leader against the evil forces that were holding China enslaved. Could he not have been a great leader, following along the lines of a wide leadership control, he would have been, at least, a ready Dare-to-Die, glad to throw his life into any balance that would favor the land of his forebears.

As it was, fortune had favored him. He was placed at last in that environment which, of all others, was to develop his spirit of leadership.

As a Chinese he was not submerged in Honolulu as he would have been had he come first to America itself. A Chinese had a greater play of employment, a larger and freer choice of vocation in Hawaii than in America. He could learn American institutions with less restriction in Honolulu than in San Francisco or New York. He was not only welcome but needed in Hawaii, and hence was respected. The Chinese thrives only where he is respected. He will not stay where he is not wanted. Sun immediately felt at home in Honolulu. He knew that Da Ko and he were wanted there. But even in all the delight of his new environment he realized that China was, after all, the land he loved.

Every step forward that he made in his studies and his observations was a step forward on that new path that some day all Chinese were to follow —the path that showed how to build trusses of steel and shape them into a ship—and that still, amid all this wonder-work, allowed a halting on the journey of progress for the Sabbath rest.

At Honolulu, in 1879, Wen was still only a young fellow. Much of this period is now gone from his memory. But the foundation of his leadership came from the subconscious adaptation of his Chinese civilization to the new and exacting conditions of that more modern higher civilization.

He still wore his queue, and his way of thinking was still purely Chinese, but the change was gradually working over his young mind. It was a change that would make him a leader of men, and eventually the founder of the most populous republic of all time.

121

## XX

AFTER he had spent a few days in Honolulu,
seeing the sights and getting acquainted in
his new midst, Wen was conducted by his brother
to a place which he knew under the name of Ewa,
and which is now in the Pearl Harbor district.

Here Da Ko had a general merchandise store,
and here Wen was to learn the shop business.
How he did work! He soon picked up a knowledge
of the Kanaka dialect, in which he became ulti-
mately most proficient, a necessary accomplishment, for in that early period even Americans had
to speak more or less Kanaka.

He also learned how to keep the four or five
Chinese account-books, which were kept in the
usual painstaking, cumbrous Chinese fashion, in
connection with the ever-present abacus.

One thing he regretted greatly: he had no chance
to learn English at Ewa. His brother spoke English but had no time to instruct Wen, since he was
busy most of the time on his rice plantation, some
two miles from the store. The language of the

shop was Kanaka with the customers, and Cantonese when Wen and his co-workers were alone in the store.

After Wen had learned fully the details of the business he found life very monotonous. He yearned to obtain an education, of which the foundation should be a knowledge of English.

Da Ko was most generous, after the hearty Chinese fashion, and, before the arrival of young Wen, had adopted a young Chinese who was a fellow-villager and sent him to school in Honolulu. This fellow-villager had already been two years in the Bishop School at Honolulu when Da Ko decided that it was time for Wen to attend school, also. Foreign teaching had not hurt this young fellow-villager; therefore it was not bad for Wen.

Wen, therefore, entered the Honolulu English Missionary Bishop School. For ten days the teachers had him sit and watch what was going on about him. They communicated with him by signs, for he understood no English. These ten days he sat silently at his desk, but all the time his mind was reaching out toward what was going on about him. What reflections must have surged in his mind! How hard the way of learning now seemed!

Shortly after these ten days of silence, he made a startling discovery. It was not necessary to

123

learn one English word after another as he had learned Chinese, mastering thousands upon thousands of different pictural emblems. By some miraculous method, each word in English could be broken up into parts called letters and saved to be used again in making up another word in a most wondrous fashion. It was like eating your cake and still having it. Ah! here was the beginning of the "clearer life."

In addition to this great boon of the alphabet he found there was a great advantage in being able to reason out the words. There was no reason in a Chinese ideograph. It was just a fanciful suggestion of a picture, which had to be most carefully considered in all its arbitrary details in connection with the radicals.

The discovery that English could thus be so easily acquired brought great joy to Wen, and his progress was most rapid in reading and writing English. Then came arithmetic; and his keen young mind, with memory sharpened in the Choy Hung School, made easy progress. Intuitively he had disciplined his mind in the Blue Valley school, and this discipline was now his boon.

But in the midst of his joy in the ease of acquiring knowledge through the "clearer life," there came a most excruciating period. The novelty of his appearance (with his Blue Valley gown

124

of blue, and his thick, long, shiny queue) beginning
to wear off, the older Kanaka and the half-caste
boys of the school began to amuse themselves by
pulling his queue. Wen stood it as long as he
thought prudent. Then suddenly he began a most
vigorous and open warfare of retaliative defense
upon his tormentors, both singly and collectively.
Soon he demonstrated that he was too strong for
the combined offensive of the whole crowd that
tormented him. The hard muscles, the strong
heart, the deep breath, and the heavy fists that
he had developed in the fields of Blue Valley stood
him in such good stead that finally his aggressors
left him respectfully alone. For a time he was
allowed to enjoy peace and calm. But again the
vindictiveness of his aggressors flared up. In the
humiliation of their defeat the older gang of
school-boys decided upon the safer policy of passing the game of queue-pulling along to the
younger lads. These they accordingly urged on to
renew the exasperating and painful teasing of
Wen. The strategy of this issue as thus developed
was a hard one for the young Chinese student.
He could fight and beat off the older boys, but he
immediately realized that it would not be just to
hurt the little fellows, who, after all, were only
acting under the guidance of the older pupils. It
was a difficult situation for the emigrant, still a

stranger in a strange land. It was not in his nature to hurt the weak, and so he allowed the small boys to brutally tease him and cruelly wrench his queue with impunity, until they themselves became tired of the torture and eventually left him alone.

I think that the queue episode explains much of the reason for Sun's great power of leadership. He thrashed all the older boys for those cruel wrenchings of his hair, fought them single-handed, individually and collectively; and when the older boys, beaten and cowed, bethought themselves of the unfair and cowardly attack through the younger lads, even these Wen finally subdued by substituting patience for his strong fists.

Wen simply did not have it in his heart to beat up the younger boys as he had the older, and the spirit that made him brave in withstanding the treacherous pulls at his queue was the same spirit that outwitted the strength of an empire. In other words, Wen was a tactician, and he changed his tactics of force for the extreme of diplomacy in the school-ground, just as in after years, after an armed effort, he would spend months—and even years—of cautious waiting before he used again the force of armed violence.

He studied his man just as Spartacus, the hero of the Roman arena, watched and waited for the chance to strike when he knew the weak points of his adversary. Like a champion of the boxing-ring, if he could not wear his adversary down with blows he would wear him out with endurance.

At Honolulu in those days there was a wonderful swimming-pool of clear, deep water on the path that led to the Pali, and there the boys of the Honolulu school were wont to go for a swim. Here again Wen frequently had to demonstrate his strength, notwithstanding his victory over the queue-pullers, in encounters with more or less racial sentiment as their incentive, arising from swimming in the pool, in which outsiders—much older boys—were involved. But finally by common consent, half-castes, Kanakas and foreigners, accepted him, queue and all, and made him one of them. At last he had won their admiration and favor in his long struggle for self-respect.

School-boy teasing was not the only trouble that centered about his queue. He was continually asked by friendly foreigners:

"Why don't you cut off your pigtail?"

This was a question in which he himself at length joined. He gathered some of the other Chinese into his confidence and told them of his own troubles with his queue, but he declared that no Chinese should cut off his queue until *all* were ready to cut off the emblem of Chinese self-respect. He declared that the queue was a political badge, and accordingly all Chinese should act together in what concerned it; cutting off the queue might save one Chinese much teasing and abuse, but it would not better the condition of all Chinese, and would make the foreigner believe that the Chinese were ashamed of being Chinese.

"Let us band ourselves together with the eventual aim of cutting off our queues when all Chinese cut off *their* queues," was his youthful injunction. "If we, one by one, cut them off, then we lose our national type and become mere wanderers, ashamed to go home and ashamed to stay abroad. This foolish custom, forced on us by the Manchus, must be borne by us until all Chinese make up their minds to throw it aside, or at least gather in sufficient number to make a showing to the world. Besides," further declared the young reformer, "the queue is but one of the disgraces which China suffers, and we should try to overcome them all at once by concerted action."

It was, however, only in 1895, at Yokohama, that he cut off his queue, largely to help in his disguise in revolutionary work.

And now that he knew English his school became his wonderland. Great, indeed, was his interest in the school fire brigade. In his native village he recalled how fire meant the greatest confusion, since there was no preparation for the emergency of conflagrations; but here again the foreigners were superior. About the third school year military drill was also introduced, which gave him great delight. He took most active interest in the drills and exercises that were held in the school compound and became proficient in military tactics, a proficiency of great help later in his revolutionary years.

The three years he spent at this school thoroughly modernized him and made him yearn for the awakening of China. He had observed painstakingly every school discipline. So assiduous was he in his studies and so successful in their pursuit that he received at his graduation, from the hand of Kalakua, then king of the Hawaiian Islands, a prize. This prize was awarded to him for excellence in English literature, and I presume that the amiable king had some difficulty in selecting a prize that would fit the occasion. The king finally selected for Wen, as his prize, a book on China. From those ten days of silence Wen had struggled on to be the first in his class in the foreign language that he now knew perfectly, both in its written and spoken use.

I have often wondered at the most masterly command Sun Yat Sen has of English, and his fluency in the shading of words for exact expression of meaning. His pronunciation in English runs rather to the American than to the English style. Cantonese have more difficulty in pronouncing the English letter "r" than do some other Chinese provincials, for they have no equivalent phonetic for this consonant. Thus they employ the nearest phonetic in their dialect, which happens to be "l." Hence, ordinarily they say "gleat" instead of "great," "velly" instead of "very," etc. Wen, I know, right from the beginning, never had any of this difficulty, since he has such a close appreciation of phonetics.

The only time I ever knew the doctor to go back to idiomatic Chinese in the use of English was when he was telling me one day of his difficulties in June of 1918, in opening the regular parliament of the Republic. Mok Yung Sing was substituted as acting governor in Canton and promised to obey Sun's orders as President of China. Mok, however, secretly conspired against Sun. Consequently, Sun ordered a couple of gunboats to proceed against Mok.

"As often as the shots struck the yamen, Mok came to apologize," quietly remarked Sun in the quick narration of the dramatic situation. I understood the idiom and paid no attention to its use (O-men hwei hwei da ta-dy yamen, ta whei hwei chuh lai kiang). Of course, the idiom, as the Chinese use it, meant an intensive emphasis. Sun, however, immediately corrected it by saying:

"Mok lost no time in coming to apologize."

This was the only time that I ever knew Sun to make even an approach to a mistake in his use of standardized English.

Despite the fact that Cantonese and Mandarin were the languages in which he had to do most of the work of thirty years' effort in founding the Republic, Sun Yat Sen has freed his English from all errors, even to those which are necessarily excusable by the extreme variance of the tongues he uses. Needless to state, this linguistic accomplishment had its foundation in his devotion to his studies in Honolulu.

After graduating from the Bishop School with first honors, he attended to the business affairs of his brother for half a year, after which he attended a higher school in Honolulu then called the St. Louis School. Here he studied for a term, finally pursuing his studies in the Hawaii College.

At this time a most serious situation arose. Da Ko, as a Chinese irrevocably wedded to custom, did not want Wen's Ocean-man education to interfere with his adherence to the exactions of ancient learning. He believed that Wen had had enough, for his own good, of foreign teaching when he graduated from the Bishop School and did not want him to be spoiled by further foreign teachings. For Da Ko, in spite of all his shrewd business acumen and sterling qualities, was still a willing slave to the ancient institutions of China. He did not want Wen to be un-Chinafied, foreignized, or modernized any further. Any one familiar with Chinese life will appreciate Da Ko's attitude toward his younger brother in this regard, in a way hard to explain to others.

Therefore, Da Ko decided that Wen had had enough of foreign teaching and that he should return to China. The younger brother was deeply grieved at this announcement. He, however, did not question the right of Da Ko to decide this all-important matter. Under Da Ko's command Wen sailed back to the family circle in the Blue Valley.

But he went back a new being. He was barely eighteen, but he felt that the mantle of full manhood had fallen upon him; and it was not the manhood of ancient China looking ever backward into the misty past for those models of the ancients. It was the manhood of a new China; a new China in whose making he would, by the Providence of God, play the chief part.

# THIRD PERIOD

1884 to 1886

ENGLISH INFLUENCE AT HONG KONG AFTER THE
"WASTED YEAR"

## XXI

UNDER the stern command of Da Ko, Wen, his heart saddened by disappointment, made the long journey back from Honolulu to China. Deep, indeed, was his disappointment in not being able to complete fully all the educational courses available in Hawaii. He comforted himself with the thought that at all events he was well entered upon the "clearer life." Fortified with his Occidental start in education, Wen now resolved to take every opportunity to help in the reformation of Chinese political conditions. He was then eighteen years of age. His first opportunity to attempt a preachment of reform came before he had landed at his home town in China.

Being obliged to disembark at Hong Kong from the ship which had brought him from Honolulu, in order to make connection with a native junk sailing for Choy Hung, he eagerly seized this his first opportunity at reform among strangers.

The Chinese customs service had to be passed at the little island of Cap Suy Mun at the mouth

135

of the Hong Kong Harbor. As the junk approached the island the junk captain, having daily experience with the independent character of his fellow-Chinese, drew all the passengers together and admonished:

"Make no trouble or expostulation with these custom or *likin* officers. If you do it will go hard with you."

The passengers all quietly submitted to the exactions made of them. Wen also, in order to avoid giving trouble to the ship's master, submitted to the arrogant and undue impositions made by the officers, who were more intent on getting their "squeeze" than on complying with the duties of their office. Many of the passengers were compelled to make involuntary presents to the greedy officials to avoid confiscation of their chattels, and perchance to save themselves from fines and arrest.

Having, as he thought, fully satisfied the officials, Wen repacked and strapped his baggage. But no sooner had he locked up his belongings than another set of harpies appeared.

"Open up your baggage."

"I have already passed the examination," declared Wen. "Why do you wish to cause me the trouble and annoyance of another examination?"

"That examination was only for the native customs. We appear for the *likin* dues," the crafty officers insisted.

To this Wen made no answer but opened up his belongings. The second examination effected, he packed up, strapped, and locked his baggage as before. A while passed; then a third set of officials appeared on the deck, their swords rattling as they prowled about. They came to Wen.

"Open up!"

"Already I have passed two examinations," declared Wen.

"Oh, that was only for the native customs and the *likin*," contemptuously declared the new set of officials. "We are the officers who protect the people against opium smuggling."

For the third time Wen allowed his baggage to be ransacked. Another period of waiting passed. After Wen had for the third time put his baggage in condition for a continuance of the voyage, behold a fourth set of officials appear! Uniformed and armed.

"Open up!" they commanded.

"And why do you now come?" asked Wen. "Are not three examinations sufficient?"

"No," declared the chief of the fourth set of officials. "We are the authorities who protect the public against kerosene smuggling. Make no delay in opening up your trunks and bags, so that we may see if you are smuggling any kerosene.''

''But this is nonsense!'' declared Wen. ''You well know from the amount, the size and appearance of my luggage that I have no room therein to store or smuggle kerosene. Why, then, should you bother me with this senseless demand?''

Thereupon the officials threatened. But Wen was obdurate. He refused to submit to their demands in such terms that at length the greedy officials were cowed.

Whereupon the other passengers came and pleaded with him.

''Let this examination be made also, for if you do not they will keep us here unduly and without reason,'' they pleaded. Still Wen would not submit to the imposition, thinking it an auspicious occasion to begin the practice of his reform.

Then the captain of the junk came and growled.

''I am sorry for you and the passengers,'' returned Wen. ''But I shall make amends when we arrive in port by helping you appeal your case (if you can) to higher officials, who, if they are just, will see that these men are punished for their organized conspiracy to extort from the public by their progressive system of corrupt examination.''

At this the junk captain laughed.

"And do you not know that there is no such thing as an appeal to higher authority in China? And if you should go to the higher officials, they, too, would only make more trouble for us."

According to the forecast of the junk captain, the junk passengers did have trouble; for the officials kept the junk there all the rest of that day and the succeeding night and well into the next morning, when the captain was made to pay bribe money that the combined set of officials blandly called a "fine."

Wen, however, took advantage of the situation by preaching to the passengers the need of a political reform in China.

"Will you continue to be indifferent," he asked, "when China is in the grip of official corruption and vice?" Up to the last hour, when the old junk finally landed him at Kam Shing anchorage, he worked among the passengers, trying to make converts to reform.

From Kam Shing, Wen proceeded up the river to his home in Blue Valley, where, after the feasting and rejoicing were at an end, he entered upon a period which he described to me as his "wasted year"; for in Blue Valley he had to abandon further attempt at progress in Occidental learning. I do not consider, however, that the year was wasted. It seems to me that this year was one of the most fruitful of his whole life, for in it he commenced to have confidence in his own ability to bring about reform. Hardly had the home-coming feast terminated than we find him addressing certain of the village as follows:

"Why," he bravely uttered, "should you address prayers phrased to the government at Peking in the choicest figures of language? Do you think that they are read? Do you believe that they have one honest moment's attention? You praise in your petitions the 'benevolence of the government and the grace of the emperor.' Where is there anything manifest in China that shows this benevolence and grace? You declare that the Government is good but that the officials are bad. What is the difference between the two? What makes a government? When officials are corrupt, then government is also corrupt."

Hence, without knowing it, Wen had finally begun the actual work of a plan to overthrow that corrupt government which had weighed so hard upon the people that he loved. Even though it would cause, within the period of the "wasted year," heartbreaks in the family circle, the family circle which he loved so well.

## XXII

### YAMEN RUNNING TO A TOWN OF IGNORANCE

IN CONSIDERING this very important period of the Reformer's "wasted year," it may be well to reflect upon his mental attitude on his return to Honolulu. This return, except for the Manchu *likin* thieves incident, was uneventful, save for the revolutionary effect of his own reveries, as he found himself sailing back over those summer seas to the Blue Valley hamlet of his birth.

He knew that the purple heights of the Plowshare Mountains would be there to greet him, emblematic of that rude labor of the fields in which his own hands from babyhood had had their share. Yes, and the village itself would be unchanged except for a new building here and there, built ever stronger and higher in the fear of those attacks of the river pirates that he knew likewise would still continue to menace the hamlet.

In his mind's eye he pictured the school in the

141

village temple and heard the high drone of the pupils led on by the higher pitch of the teacher as they sang on in that eternal chorus:

"When man begins, all good by nature, nature always near, Practice always far. If without teaching, nature will change. Teaching with doctrine, man always right. Former Mencius living,
Select neighbors living." [1]

It may be here remarked that the method of teaching this classic was the method of the whip. *Giao puh ien sz-dz-go* (teach not severe, teacher wrongs). The ancient idea of teaching was to thresh it in. If a character was forgotten the rod was applied. This was indorsed by the maxim above quoted, which more liberally rendered is: "If the teaching is not severe, the teacher's inability is seen." It was only by this heroic method that the Chinese boys could be made to absorb wisdom.

Yes, it was a hodgepodge compared to the Ocean-men's easy method, but it gave something that the Ocean-men could not find in the pliancy of their alphabet. It gave that touch of mystery to letters that led the true scholar into the deepest recesses of that far-away philosophy of con-

[1] This is a literal translation of the first words of the three-syllable classic, which, fully expressed, would be something like:

Men, one and all, in infancy are virtuous at heart.
Their moral tendencies the same, their practices far apart,
    etc., etc.

tent; and now this hodgepodge formulated itself
into:

Men, one and all in infancy are virtuous at heart.
Their moral tendencies the same, their practices wide apart,
    etc.

And now this mystery of the Chinese classics
was his, for he had kept up his Chinese reading
even during those years away from China, and the
golden key that had opened up these mysteries
was the art and science that he had learned in the
Land of the Clearer Life beyond.

Yes, the temple school was now dear to him, for
it was the first fountain of his learning, into which
had dripped the noisome superstition of those
three painted gods that stood by the Blue Valley
school, itself poisoning the very spring that fed
the fountain of ancient wisdom.

There was much to shock Wen's nature in the
immediate days that followed his home-coming,
but it made him resolute in his determination to
show others the way of that "clearer life" that he
had just left.

Now, returned as a young man of eighteen, he
still had no voice in the council of the village
elders. He knew that whatever he would say in
protest at the ignorance and superstition that surrounded him would be attributed to the poisonous
effect of foreign teaching and the temerity of

youth. Still, it was his duty to speak. So he uttered his protests, one sacrilege after another, until the village elders wagged their heads in doubt and then shook them in anger at his utterances against the good old ancient Chinese way.

Had not Wen, from his earliest boyhood, been looked upon with favor in Blue Valley, the hard hands and strong muscles of the villagers would have given him short shrift, for, verily, never had anything so wicked been pronounced against the sacred customs of China.

"Worshipful Heaven!" they exclaimed. "Has anything so felonious ever been spoken?" Sun's attitude in the village midst could only be likened to the cowboy of the West standing up in the climax of the Sunday sermon and cursing the preacher to the accompaniment of a few revolver-shots at the chandelier.

From household to household the people of Blue Valley discussed the madness of this lad of whom they had all been so fond. Ah, it was well that his elder brother Da Ko had made him come back from that ruinous country, where men were taught to dishonor the land of their ancestors. Perhaps, after all, he might mend his ways and be cured of the madness he had contracted in the land of the Ocean-men. In the hope that he would eventually repent, and likewise under the fear of of-

144

Dr. Sun (center) about the time of his first onslaught on the Canton Yamen during the ninth Moon of 1895.

"DARE-TO-DIE," for China.

fending one on whom they were already beginning, in spite of themselves, to look upon as a leader, they listened to him. It was all sacrilege and nonsense, but still they listened. Now it was the district yamen that came in for abuse.

"Your district yamen is in the city of Sheang Shan. Well, what does your yamen do for you? Once a year the yamen runner comes here to Choy Hung to collect the amount of money which the district yamen says that you should pay. And when he has obtained your money, he goes his way, and you ask nothing from him, and he asks nothing more from you."

As Wen spoke thus, the crowd of villagers gathered closely about him. He went on:

"The yamen runner does not even speak to you of any affair, no matter how great its importance, that has happened in the whole year in your village. Your district yamen and the runner and the people from the neighboring towns about know nothing and ask nothing of you and of your town. Why? Because you are not any better than the district yamen, for you will not let the district yamen interfere in your affairs, and the district yamen will not let you interfere in its affairs. So there you have a deadlock. They get your money, and you get nothing for it. A government should take care of all things for the people, just as the

145

master of the house takes care of each member of the household.

"If you want a road, you have to build it yourself and by your own labor, or by a subscription among yourselves. You even have to build from your own pockets the bridges that the Manchu soldiers use. It is true that here we do not need cart-roads, for we have but few carts. We do, however, need bridle-paths, and since these bridle-paths lead out to the roads, we should likewise encourage the building of cart-roads. Your taxes should show something each year, in schools and bridges and roads. Where does your tax money go? To the Son of Heaven. What does the Son of Heaven do for you in this Choy Hung hamlet? Nothing. This 'Son of Heaven' government is so rotten that you don't want to have anything to do with its officials. You pay these taxes in order that they shall leave you alone. You know that it is cheaper for you to build your own roads and bridges and maintain your own schools [2] than to let the Manchus come in for their added squeeze."

Wen also called their attention to the slight intercourse that the people of his hamlet had with the outside world, and bemoaned the fact that there was nothing to connect up his hamlet with

---

[2] Each head of the family contributed according to the number of the children from that family.

the world about, all because of the indifference of the Manchus and the retaliatory spirit of the Chinese villagers.

He spoke of the advantage that might be obtained from the market fairs which rotated from one village to another in the whole region of the valleys about. These periodical village markets were curiously named for the dates on which they were held. The one to the north of Blue Valley was called "The Two-five-eight Day Market"; the one to the south, "The One-four-seven Day Market"; and the one to the east, "The Four-three-nine Day Market"; the numbers indicating the days of the moons in which the markets were held. In every moon there were nine days of market in the district covering these three villages. Through the medium of these markets the people could get together for mutual benefit and progressive action.

"You should use these markets so that each town may benefit by its intercourse with the others," declared Sun. "Not one of these three towns has anything to hold up as a model to the others, for you are all in an ignorant and superstitious rut. You are starting for nowhere and do not get very far at that. Why do you not wake up and remember that men can better their condition only by combined and honest efforts?"

Such was the sense of the political preachings

147

that young Wen would make on every appropriate occasion. Many listened to him, convinced of his reasoning.

"You are not to be blamed," he would say. "Your so-called Son of Heaven is the one at fault. A government should, at least, give its citizens some basis of convenience for its trade. What regard do you pay to the stamp of the coins of the Manchus? You have to weigh every piece. Even these silver dollars that have come from the Philippines and from Mexico—these very dollars, good in other countries—you cut up and weigh out into a mutilated yet honest coinage of your own, for the Manchus give you no fair coinage, and even the copper cash has to be weighed regardless of what the figure on it may state to be its value.

"Not only do the Manchus do nothing for you politically, but they neglect all moral teaching. There is no attempt to improve the public morals. You all still believe in that foolish doctrine of *feng sui*. How can there be such a doctrine as that of the wind and the waters?"

This sort of activity in argument would sometimes be accompanied by a practical illustration to incite interest in political information.

Taking a cash (a copper coin worth then about a twentieth of a cent), Wen would ask:

"Who is the ruler of China?"

"Why, the Son of Heaven is the ruler of China," would come the ready response.

"Is this Son of Heaven a Chinese?"

"Of course; none save a Chinese is fit to be the Son of Heaven."

"Then behold on this coin the characters that are prescribed by the one you call the Son of Heaven. See, the characters are not Chinese; they are Manchu. China is not ruled by the Chinese but by the Manchus." And he would show his proposed convert the "black" side of the coin, which was in Manchu, on the other, the "white" side, being the Chinese characters.

So dense was the ignorance of the masses that many of them did not know that the Manchu was a foreign ruler; for the only authorities who represented that power with whom they came in contact in such small villages were Chinese. For example, the chief representative in the hamlet of the Son of Heaven was the *tippao*.

The *tippao* was the supervisor of the village affairs under the direction of the village elders. He was responsible for the good conduct of the town peace, and was the intermediary between the mandarins and other outside officials. The *tippaos* also served as official witnesses, approaching, in effect, the identification office of a notary.

In Choy Hung the village supplied five policemen to assist the *tippao* in keeping order. They
were paid by the village elders on a sort of village
communal agreement, their pay being in kind,
from grain, or in a certain percentage of the crops
per *mow*.

In some of the larger towns the office of *tippao*
is lucrative, but in Choy Hung the office was of so
much bother and of so little profit that no one
wanted it. Hence, recourse had to be made to the
drawing of lots at the village temple to ascertain
whom the gods made the unlucky man.

The *tippao* of Choy Hung, as guardian with his
five policemen of the whole hamlet, had a full-sized
job on his hands, for he had to guarantee every
villager that he would protect his house and build-
ings from fire and his fields from being robbed
and pilfered. He, therefore, constituted a sort of
insurance company, the small reward given him
for such service being an insurance premium.
And generally he made a good insurance company,
since the only way he could get a reward and avoid
loss was the taking care of the homes and crops
of his subscribers.

I doubt if Wen could have found a more auspicious and indulgent place for his first attempts
at reform than in the little town of Blue Valley,
which, having no official standing, had no connec-

tion with the outside world. It was a solitary little
town, taking care of itself as best it could, and
hence not under the cloud of the larger effort of
the Son of Heaven to hold the fear of his authority ever over the people. The petty official world
of Heang Shang and of the nearest *likin* post
(nearly as far off as Hong Kong) never heard of
the preachings of reform practised by Wen on the
simple villagers of Choy Hung, preachings that
would have brought him to the torture-rack even
at that early age if he had been where Manchu
officials could have informed themselves of his
rebellion against the rule of the Son of Heaven.

However, during the whole of this "wasted
year" that Wen spent at Choy Hung, his courage
grew in its sympathy for the simple folk of the
village, who acknowledged the Son of Heaven as
their master, well knowing that the only solicitude of their Son of Heaven was to get those bags
of well-worn copper and mutilated silver which
the *tippao*, as the only connecting link between
Blue Valley and the world beyond, lugged out
periodically to Heang Shang as a tribute so that
Blue Valley might be left alone.

Likewise, during this "wasted year" his mind
lay like a field, waiting fallow for the planting of
the seed of the next springtime.

## XXIII

AMONG the treasured books that Sun carried back with him from Honolulu to China was the Bible.

Christianity had become to him a great institution for civilization. It was a tree that bore fruits ever ripening on the highways of the brotherhood of man to be plucked by all, regardless of race or other conditions.

By contrasting his own Chinese civilization with that of the Christian, he beheld the disadvantage which China suffered in not possessing a progressive religion. He looked at Christianity from the practical viewpoint of its results. He saw that it continued to grow up with the advancing demands of ever-modernizing civilization, while Confucianism, Buddhism, and Taoism held the Chinese back to the standards set two thousand and more years before.

He discovered seeming inconsistencies in the Old Testament and as many more in the Gospels, but these suggested weaknesses were mere chaff in his mind, swept away by Christ's wonder philosophy that had built up the world into new races of men.

Sun Yat Sen is not a dreamer as many suppose. He is most intensely practical. His philosophy is the philosophy of the plow as it turns up its furrow, and not that of the birds that scatter seed in their flight. Therefore, Christianity appealed to him because it had accomplished practical wonders that he could never have believed, had he not seen them himself. He saw that it, disciplined men, made them single heads of wholesome families, reduced their weaknesses, and added to their strength. To him, at that early and susceptible period of his life in the Hawaiian schools, the teachings of the Nazarene were at the foundation of that great edifice of knowledge that taught men the way of a pure wisdom within the reach of all.

He recalled the beauties of the teachings and lessons of Confucius and of Mencius. He could understand now these phrasings which, at first, in the village school had been so incoherent to his comprehension.

Unlike many other lads taught in the village school, he had, at length, drawn a sweet philosophy from those classical golden texts. He believed thoroughly in the Chinese *theory* of morality, but

153

he saw that its practice was not possible, since there was no guide to bring it down to the exactions of the new times. The old Chinese masters had weighed their wisdom in the scales of a time so far spent and gone that now no true and skilled hand survived to show even the true marking of the balance. Hence, in his ardent admiration for Christianity Wen felt no derogation for the philosophy of his own race. That rich philosophy of the old Chinese searchers for truth had endured too long not to have its merit, but the cutting edge of its instrument had been blunted by too long use.

Wen's mind was very appreciative of the rare philosophy of Confucius and the other classic masters. The imported Buddhism of China he regarded with respect, but he bemoaned the ignorance of Taoism. To him as a boy the worship in the native village temple seemed to be a debased mixture of the last two cults, of neither of which had he any special information, since to the town it was merely the "good joss." The painted gods in this village temple that he had known from his babyhood had no priests to attend them nor to explain their meaning. When a villager was in hard luck, Wen knew that the unlucky one went to the village temple to "chin-chin the joss." Beyond this vague reflection the temple of his village was a mere rubbish-receptacle for the

154

three painted gods that were on certain rare occasion paraded through the town.

As previously stated, Choy Hung had never even been visited by missionaries; but in Honolulu Wen had come to know missionaries—good missionaries—who preached and practised the gospel of the Golden Rule. The truth of those teachings he accepted. Why not? There were the proofs on every hand to show that they were living truths that could be practised.

He reasoned that there had to be a foundation for every structure of reason. What foundation was there on which the Chinese people could build up a newer civilization that would make the world respect their race? Was it to be the foundation of religion?

He now realized that by the command of his elder brother Da Ko he had been made to return from Honolulu to a land of ignorance, and that that land was China, the land of his forebears. He loved China in spite of its superstition and ignorance. Again and again would he try to excuse Chinese shortcomings by saying: "The Chinese are old-fashioned. They only follow ancient customs, many of which are good."

Finally there came a time when he could no longer excuse all those customs. Foot-binding, concubinage, opium-smoking, lack of sanitation,

155

corruption among officials—these could not be excused on the ground of custom. Hence, as he came homeward he felt that he was going to a strange and darkened land. The institutions of the land of progress that he was leaving had become more his own than were even those of China, the land of his birth.

He knew that his father would oppose his continuing his foreign education, for his father, like all other old-time Chinese, believed in the time-honored Chinese rule of looking backward rather than forward for models of learning. His father was afraid of the strange forward and changeful teaching of the Occident. His father wanted Wen to be honored in his own home town.

"Wen could never be honored in Choy Hung," thought the father, "if he did not respect the ancient institutions of China—yes, even respect the gods of the village temple."

His father was getting old, very old. He was too old to work. Wen tried to excuse Da Ko's stern command to return to Choy Hung upon the ground that filial obedience exacted his presence to honor his father and his mother. He did indeed honor his parents, but, alas, it was not long before his conduct began to worry those whom he would honor. Even as Wen went about the village preaching reform, his family forgave him; forgave him up to the very hour of that final abomination to be committed by Wen in the very presence of the village temple itself. An abomination which is worth narration.

From his earliest recollections Wen had been taken by his mother or father—or both—to prostrate himself before the three idols of the village temple. These three idols were as familiar to him as the faces of the family in his own household. There was the Northern Emperor, he of the beard and the savage grin. To his right was the Queen of Heaven, with a flowing gown and gorgeous headdress; and to his left was the Mother Goddess, she whose smile was more subdued, and to whose shrine came the women of the village to pray for themselves and their children.

He had been taught not only to prostrate himself but likewise to pray before these idols; but it was a mere mumbling of form, and more like a nursery rime than a prayer. Yet even upon his return from Honolulu his father, his mother and every member of the family found their only expression of spiritual relief in prostrations, incense-burning and joss word-mumbling before the throne of that god of wood and paint and his consorts.

On his return from Honolulu he had noticed that the temple was growing ramshackle and abandoned, and the great curved roof of tile and bright red bricks showed signs of decay. But the idols themselves were brightly and newly painted, and he knew the day would come when the temple itself would again be put in order and made to do honor to the town. All respectable villages had to have a temple, just as every reputable town of the West had to have its church.

He knew that there was no one to profit from the temple except the old gate-keeper who, at any hour of the day or night, would always open, glad to get the well-deserved pittance of a few cash that the worshiper would pay for the joss-paper and incense. There was no priest, no ritual; it was a salvation-free proposition for anyone who wanted to enjoy the blessings of the three idols.

Ah, there was the trouble, in bringing about a reform against superstition! The Chinese customs were all founded upon convenience, and it was so convenient and inexpensive to have these town idols, which one could worship or not as he wished, without any substantial expense. It was a free-for-all expression of good will toward the spirits, and even the foreigner (if there had been any) could worship these gods free of charge. It was a sort of spiritual town pump at which all might draw without let or hindrance according to need.

As a child, he had seen the Northern Emperor

—he who was carved out of solid oak and painted like a circus-wagon—paraded through the streets with salutes of giant firecrackers. It had pleased him then, as a child, and he thought that he understood the story of the Northern Emperor (and his two consort goddesses to do him honor) as a western child learns the story of "Jack the Giant-killer."

Wen had often thought of these painted gods while in school at Honolulu. His teachers had asked him about his village temple, and he had told them. To him, this temple, with its three idols, stood as a symbol of China's distress. He felt that the Chinese people wanted to go forward but that they would never progress as long as they pinned their spiritual confidence on joss-paper and painted gods. He believed that this idolatry was the very foundation of ignorance. Back in Honolulu in the cheerful midst of the Sunday-school he used to see in his memory the painted smile of the Northern Emperor, and he learned to know that it was the painted smile of the wooden idol that was holding China back. Hence, these gods of the village temple immediately upon Wen's return became very irritating to him. It distressed him to think that his father, and his mother as well, should pray and prostrate themselves before those miserable blocks of carved

159

and painted wood. He repeated to himself that there could be no advance in China before this mental confusion of worship and its shackling influence of superstition was done away with.

"Superstition makes men afraid," he declared. "These painted images, set up in all parts of China, must first come down before China can become a progressive nation. For superstition means fear and ignorance."

One day he led some of his companions to the village temple and went up to the great wooden god, the Northern Emperor. The Northern Emperor was grinning as usual and looked quite lifelike. Some of Wen's companions commenced to "chin-chin" the god. Wen pushed them back and made them stand up. Then he reached up and seized hold of one of the wooden fingers of the Northern Emperor. The lads about stood aghast at the sacrilege.

"Why should we worship gods of wood in this village?" he cried out. "They cannot even help themselves! Who, then, shall say that they can help us? Now look and see if the god can prevent me while I twist off his finger. Watch sharp to see if he even winces."

With that Wen gave a great twist at the big wooden finger of the Northern Emperor and, after hard wrenching and pulling, broke it off.

Pathway to a Confucian temple. ". . . the majestic stream of Confucius's teaching, which, however, reached no Ocean of Science and touched no Shore of Progress" (Page 362).

"How much like China were those clumsy, keelless junks . . . Why should China always continue the snail-like pace of the junk?" (Page 171.)

Holding the finger up before his companions he declared:

"Now you see the sort of god that you have to protect your village! I break and twist his finger off, and he holds his grins the same as before. What sort of a god is that to protect the village?"

His companions all fled from the temple, terror-stricken and horrified at the sacrilege.

In a short time the news went forth through the whole village. Wen's name was anathematized. Fathers advised their sons:

"Keep away from that mad boy. That is what foreign teaching does. Such sacrileges are only taught by the Ocean-men. This abomination may bring us all bad luck."

His parents were almost heartbroken at the news, although, against the angry protestations of the neighbors, they stood, Chinese fashion, firm for their boy, both to "save their own faces" and to save his. Among themselves, however, they agreed that this sacrilege was the limit of all forbearance.

After Wen's father had succeeded in appeasing the first wrath of the village elders by immediately arranging for the repair of the idol, he was compelled to agree to banish Wen from the village, whose temple the young man had so flagrantly dishonored.

Of course, it was indifferent to the village elders where Wen should be banished, so long as he was compelled by his family to leave the town immediately. Wen's genius for diplomacy finally settled the matter, and, after long-sustained debate, the family council decided that his banishment from Blue Valley should be effected by his going to Hong Kong. Eventually he secured the family council's further permission to enter Queen's College in Hong Kong.

Now that it was rumored about the hamlet that Wen was to be banished to Hong Kong, a slight reaction of sentiment showed itself in his favor. Even the women and children went to the temple to examine the injury done. Yes, it is true that Wen had mutilated the god. Wen, poisoned with the learning of the foreigner, had dishonored his own village and was, therefore, about to be driven away as one unworthy to enjoy the benefits of respectable and law-abiding Blue Valley.

Wen, the lovable, the respected comrade, the brightest classicist in the town! Wen, who honored his father and mother, the pet of the family circle . . . he had fallen, he was lost, he was driven out, back to the foreigners, since he was a menace to the peace and happiness of the hamlet of his birth. Ah, verily the curse of the gods fell upon those who dishonored the Northern Emperor! Now he would pay for all his sacrileges by being compelled to go back to the midst of the foreigners. Again it was a demonstration of the efficacy of the village gods; they were good, they never failed.

However, some of the Blue Valley villagers really felt sorry for Wen when he was driven out into that night of a most condign punishment. Nothing is more terrible to the Chinese than banishment, and to the simple villagers who lived beneath the great shadow of the Plowshare Mountain Wen was condemned most condignly.

Can we not imagine Wen, as he stood in the midst of that family circle which now he was to leave practically forever? There is something of weeping and something of tender hands held out to hold him back, for to the simple-hearted women of the family Wen is going out to a punishment almost as terrible as that of the execution-ground itself. The old father looks dubiously at his son. Da Ko sent Wen back from the Ocean-men's land to reform his ways, and Wen had only come back to Blue Valley to commit the greatest sacrilege ever known in its midst. His banishment commences with the boat that leaves at dawn. But there is no sleep for the members of that family circle. Even the departure of the two lost brothers was not attended by such anxiety as is this;

for now the honor of the family is involved. . . .
Wen must mend his ways. Since he will not obey
the precepts of Chinese wisdom, let him go forth
among the foreigners, and eventually return
humble and contrite. Foreign ways are bad, but
since he has followed them, let him keep on until,
in the wisdom of a changed mind, he repent of his
folly and come back to do honor to his family and
his village. Besides, there is no other place for
him to go; no Chinese village wants him.

Wen hears their admonition and listens to their
counsel in silence. Among his small belongings is
a Bible. He takes it out, and in the glow of the
small oil-lamp he reads silently to himself.

His mind travels over the rolling ocean to that
Land of Wondrous Promise. . . . He sees the
deep, blue Sea of Galilee, the green and glorious
Mount of Olives, the drab of lonely Moab, the
milk-white waters of the Jordan, and the ashy
beaches of the Dead Sea. Again he hears those
tales and parables of the gentle Nazarene.

In this, his hour of disgrace, he finds himself
following closer in the wanderings of the gentle
Galilean than ever before. He now feels that he
belongs to that newer and better life for which
Christ stood. The blasphemy and sacrilege in the
village temple has raised a barrier between the
China of the old and the China of to-morrow, and

164

Wen now feels that he is a part of that New China. The breaking of a piece of painted wood, and the village rises in protest. Why? Because they know nothing of that Life of Reason for which Christ lived and died.

But it is not for the priest alone to give these teachings. More than words are needed to teach China the story of Christ's self-sacrifice. There must be the example; yea, but not the example alone of his life. Christ's life, as interpreted by the ignorance of the Chinese masses, would only mean a reversion to the painted gods of the country hamlets. First of all, there had to be an elevation of the economic conditions of the masses, so that, from the higher ground of a better intelligence, they could understand the story of Him who went about doing good. Ah, yes, but a change of Chinese economic conditions meant force, meant arms, meant a relentless struggle to the very death with the evil grip that was strangling China! And this was not Christ's example —Christ, the Preacher of Love and Peace.

China did not know Christ, and Christ had never known China, but Christ was right because He had founded a civilization that had made one whole side of the world better than the other. The painted idols of the Chinese hamlets were there long before the Star of Bethlehem gleamed in the morning sky, but the painted idols still leered out from the village temples of Blue Valley, because China had never learned the story of the Child who was born in the manger. Christ's story had given the world a spiritual guide that never before had been known. It was both the chart and the compass. Yes, but all this was conjecture as regarded Wen. What could a disappointed and disgraced lad of eighteen do to show that he was struggling for better things for the land he loved?

Disgraced, banished, homeless, he was going forth into the mystery of another Ocean-men's land. Da Ko would not take him back to the fair islands of the Pacific, and Blue Valley was driving him out. He must make himself somewhere and somehow a place where he could save his face and prove to his family and to his town that, after all, the foreign learning had not poisoned him like the fangs of a mad dog.

I do not think that Sun knows it, but I believe that this, his banishment from Blue Valley, was the great and crucial turning-point of his whole life. Sun, I know, suffered from this disgrace, the greatest that can befall a self-respecting Chinese lad, but I do not think he realizes to-day that out of this early suffering there sprang a

166

sweetness of self-abnegation that made him the first of the Dare-to-Dies.

However, I feel that Sun knew as he sailed away over the waters of the Golden Star, banished from his home, that the only way he could ever recover his place in the beloved family circle of Blue Valley would be when the Manchus were scourged from the crimson halls of their feasting, and the Chinese elevated to a new sense of better things.

Nor do I think that Sun knew that this banishment was the Golgotha of his whole life, for no man knows the psychology of his mind as well as the real friend, and long years of tender regard for that family circle he was then leaving have made his mind tender toward those who had decreed his banishment.

This banishment, I believe, was the bitterest and most significant that he has ever endured. Other banishments he was to know—banishments enforced with the sharp click of the rifle-bolt and the ominous gleam of the bayonet; banishments under the frowning cannon of gunboats; banishments decreed with curses, execrations, and threats of death; banishments to far-distant shores where there was not one friend to greet him—but this, the banishment from the vale of

his birth, verily, this was the Calvary through
whose suffering he was to come forth strong
and ready for his labor for the brotherhood of
his fellows.

# XXIV

### ENGLISH INFLUENCE AT QUEEN'S COLLEGE— LESSONS FROM THE FRANCO-CHINESE WAR

WE have seen how through Wen's diplomacy his banishment from Blue Valley was turned to good account by obtaining for him his great desire to pursue his foreign studies at Hong Kong.

In Honolulu Wen had been, so far as his education went, almost entirely under American influence. His first ideas of progress were taken from what he saw of American life in the Hawaiian Islands, which, although nominally under the control of a Kanaka king, had been for some time, *de facto,* dependent upon America.

He was now destined to enjoy the benefits of the civilization which had been the mother of American culture and of which America was a part. He had formed very high ideas of the English from what he had been taught concerning them by the Americans of Honolulu.

169

The environment of Hong Kong itself was an inspiration to him. The beetling cliffs and peaks, upon which were terraced the beautiful homes of the colonists, and which overlooked the water that led to the village of his birth, gave him more or less the belief that the inspiration of the English at the very door of China would prove one of the greatest elements in bringing about Chinese reconstruction.

He was now beginning to have well-defined ideas in regard to the regeneration of China. He realized that the great mistake China had made was in trying to create a world out of his own wisdom. China long ago should have joined the great family of nations, and in that way become the beneficiary of the wisdom of all the nations, while at the same time, it should have contributed progressively to the advance of the ages.

In Hong Kong he saw about him even greater evidences of the purposes of Anglo-Saxon civilization than he had observed in Honolulu. The latter was but a pretty garden compared to grandly growing Hong Kong, where ships streamed through the blue waters of its rocky cliffs, bearing the flags and messages of the nations of the earth.

Alas! modern ships of China were not among those messengers that carried the story of the

Christian nations' advance in the new world of scientific progress. The only contribution that poor old decrepit China could make toward that endless maritime pageant was the tumbling junks, derided and laughed at in the midst of that great foregathering of modern maritime life.

How much like China were those clumsy, keel-less junks, with sails like the wings of a bat! Why could not the genius of China assert itself? Why should China always continue the snail-like pace of the junk?

He met Englishmen and other Britishmen of culture. They were his teachers in the class-room. He both felt and saw the superior discernment which their minds possessed by reason of that educative process through which he himself was now going. He began to know something about the army and navy of Great Britain. He thrilled to see its soldiers on drill and on the practice march, and never tired of watching the sinister forms of those gray battle-ships that stood ready to do the bidding of commands that came from the distant center of British official life in far-away England.

It was all very wonderful to him. There was England, a tiny country whose population was not much more, perhaps, than the annual normal birth-rate of China. And see what England had done from that small home center of its native life. It had gone everywhere and accomplished miracles, in spite of the scarcity of its population, by reason of the force of its life as a nation.

He felt that there were two kinds of foreigners, one of which was an irrevocable enemy to China. This enemy was the Manchu, who borrowed his civilization from the Chinese, but who, for all that, was more foreign to the Chinese than the fair types like the British and American, French and German. He realized that, in order to overthrow the Manchus, the people must be awakened to the progress of those foreigners who sailed the great ships that coursed the harbor of Hong Kong.

Moreover, both in the college and through other pleasant social associations with the foreigners, he conceived the idea that in order to overthrow the Manchus it was necessary to obtain the sympathy and support of the Europeans and Americans, those foreigners of the Occident.

He became more and more convinced that the Manchu imperial family with its Tartar forces scattered all over China, had been working China's ruin for over two hundred years, dragging it down deeper and deeper into a depth of helpless inanition. The weaker the Manchus could make the Chinese, the stronger they themselves would become in the control of China and its riches. He recalled what the empress dowager had said:

"Ah, what a pity it is that Chinese only travel in the foreign lands! What a wrong impression they give of China, so ably ruled by ourselves, the Manchus! Would it not be better that we sent some of our own Manchus over to those countries to show that, after all, in China there are the kingly types, such as we, the Manchus."

Sun became more and more convinced that the very rulers of his country were trying to degrade it more and more. The Manchus, who numbered a scant ten millions, were forever trying to make up in trickery, knavery, and conspiracy what they lacked in numerical strength in their control of the four hundred million.

However, the Manchu policy of minority control had been developed with the cunning of a serpent. Corruption and bribery had been its chief instruments from the beginning, and now, after two centuries of crafty conspiracy by the Manchus, even the brilliancy of Chinese scholarship had been degraded into the corrupt practices of the Manchus. If the foreign Manchus were ever to be overthrown, it would not be by scholars, for these, trained in intellectual pursuits, had had as part of their training a harsh discipline to

173

Manchu control, which took away all patriotic sentiment, and left them mere literary shells.

No such movement could come *to* the Chinese people. It would have to be a movement *from* the people themselves. The rank and file still had love of country at heart. The great Taiping Rebellion, which would have succeeded but for foreign assistance given to the Manchus, showed what the people could do, once they were awakened.

But how could such a movement be started? Sun had seen opposition to any such effort dispelled in his own family. Even his broad-minded brother, Da Ko, who had had the benefits of an Occidental business education, worshiped at the shrines of the village temple and had banished his younger brother from the land of the Oceanmen so that the younger brother should return to the ignorance and superstition of the Chinese ages. There was not one in Wen's whole family who had offered him encouragement in his attempts at reform. His brother Da Ko and all the rest of the family cherished their reputations in the hamlet of Blue Valley far too much to wish to become (as they considered) political pirates (and as bad as river pirates) in opposition to the wisdom of the ancients.

Sun Yat Sen knew into what distress his brother had been thrown by reason of his (to

Da Ko) anti-Chinese learning. To this distress
there was the added chagrin brought about by
opposition against Wen in his own village, by
reason of the idol episode and his subsequent
banishment. But in this separation from his family Wen accepted his lot stoically. To him it
was the separation from the old to the new. He
felt that the "World China" had turned against
him. Consequently, he turned to that other world
that was now opening up to him. He applied
himself with new intensity to the study of its
institutions.

The Queen's College of Hong Kong, therefore,
now became for him a most attractive center for
the new life that now showed its perspective more
fully before him. Most of his teachers were English gentlemen, whereas in Hawaii the greater
number of his teachers had been American ladies.
He observed in the decorous deportment and
carefully enunciated language of these gentlemen
something that supplemented and carried further
the sympathetic and efficient work performed by
the cultured women teachers of Honolulu. He
felt that he was coming under a stern and irrevocable, yet correct and humane, influence that
meant better things for himself and his fellows.
He still wore his queue and the traditional gown
of his race, but he felt at home in the midst of
175

the disciplined environment of these English gentlemen whose ways and customs were different. There was no queue-pulling now; he had gone beyond the benches of mischief and of school-boy pranks and found himself in a mature atmosphere of those who were following the higher call of education. His heart warmed to the English as it had to the Americans. He kept up his religious associations and appreciated the value of Christian models.

Like a soldier who after long study and practice has at length mastered the manual of arms so as to have complete confidence in his weapons, Sun now began to feel at last a confidence in his ability to show others the path of the new wisdom, for, while thus enjoying a steady advance under English tutelage in the ways of the foreigner, he was by no means neglecting his study of Chinese politics, even in the pressure of his college work. He knew now that he would have to lead out in the Great Reform. At Hong Kong, Macao, and Canton he had Chinese intimates, and these he sought out as often as his college course would permit.

He was not in China at the outbreak of the Franco-Chinese War, and it was only when he was established in the college at Hong Kong that he had an opportunity to follow its progress.

Li Hung-Chang on May 17, 1884, had agreed with the French to a memorandum by which he, as Chinese plenipotentiary, pledged the Son of Heaven to withdraw all Chinese troops from the northern provinces of Tongkin, but the war continued with considerable vigor until April 6, 1885. It was during this period that Sun, being in Hong Kong, had an opportunity to discuss the news of the war as it came through the source of general information, drawn in part from the not always exact press, and in part from the tales of returned travelers and soldiers. This information concerning the progress of the war, percolating through the density of the Chinese population, came dark and clouded to Sun Yat Sen. From the very beginning, and for a long and doubtful time, he heard stories told in the rice- and tea-shops of the great success of Chinese arms. The tales of the street elaborated upon the severe defeats of the French, who had gone down in windrows of slain before the daring attacks of the Chinese. The ancient conceit of the "World China" was again enjoying one of its delusions.

And the populace embraced these delusions joyfully. "Of course," some of the village wiseacres would declare, "of course China is winning with the ease of a mighty giant. Ha! Ha! Now

177

we shall teach these Ocean-men to respect 'World China.' "

Never did Sun fail to seize the occasion of such vapid boasting to extend the propaganda of reform, which every day, he was seeing more clearly before him.

"Nonsense," he would stoutly declare. "The French have ships of iron, whereas we have nothing but clumsy junks of wood. The French have modern cannon with trained experts who know how to direct them, while our guns are hardly fit for firing a salute, and our soldiers who man them nothing but a mob! How dare you say that we are winning when it is impossible that we should win even by the wholesale slaughter of our population? How can you fight France when you do not know where France is? You say that we are winning the war, and yet we have not the strength of ships and men to search out France. Before we entered this war, should we not have prepared for it and acquainted ourselves with foreign ways so that we would have fought France by the foreign method?

"We have numbers, but mere numbers are a hindrance rather than a help in winning a war like this. And even admitting that we have driven off the French ships, this is not a victory, for victory means control. If we were really vic-

178

tors, we would be able to go to France and fight her on her own coasts and invade her own soil as she has done here in China. O poor, deluded people! You are become childish with your idols and ancient conceits. You claim to be great and powerful when you do not even have a government of your own. The Manchus, who are foreigners, rule you and rule you with corruption. You do not even know that the world is round. Why do not you learn something first of the world, and particularly about your present enemy, before you declare that you have conquered?''

About this time, on August 23, 1885, the French Admiral Courbet ascended the Min River to the Foochow Arsenal and in seven minutes of cannonading completely destroyed the Chinese fleet of eleven huge wooden war junks.

''Now will you believe that we should make ships of steel rather than wood?'' asked Sun.

To such declarations and questions as this they would frequently bring the charge that Wen was a traitor and was working to help the foreigner. However, he continued to take advantage of every opportunity to preach the necessity of reform in China, urging that victory over France would not have been a difficult matter if even a small part of China's populace had come out of the crass ignorance of the prechristian period. He bemoaned that even the excitement of the war was not waking up the Chinese to a sense of their duties to themselves and the world. Alas! they were still trusting to the ancient precepts, and too often to those silly painted gods of luck that leered in the dusty recesses of their village temples.

Then suddenly in the gloom of this uneven war there was an incident that showed that after all the Chinese were not devoid of patriotism, although held in ignorance by the tyranny of the foreign Manchus. This incident presented itself when a French cruiser, which, coming down from Taiwan, was badly damaged, put into Hong Kong for repairs. The Chinese coolies refused to work upon it on the ground that, although in a neutral port, it was an enemy ship and, when repaired, would do damage to China, their country.

This stanch stand gave young Sun definite courage in his hopes for reform. The boycott on the repair work of the cruiser showed that the patriotism of the Chinese was being properly awakened, although in a small, sluggish, and passive way. It showed that soon the transition to activity would come. That was the trouble with the Chinese people: they were too passive, too submissive. The opposition that they made was mere obstruction. This incident indicated, at all events, that the Chinese had racial cohesion. It might not have been love of country, for if they had really loved their country, with the influence of their great numbers they would not have tamely submitted to the Manchu handful of tyrants. He was doubtful how to analyze the mind of the Chinese race as it concerned China. To the Chinese, China was the world, as previously suggested in these pages. There was nothing before or after China. China was the beginning and the end. There was no Ultima Thule for China, for there was nothing beyond China at all. There were millions of Chinese who had never heard of the existence of a foreigner, for they did not know the Manchus were foreigners.

The Ocean-men foreigners at this time were merely brushing casually against the Chinese. There was no actual contact, no meeting of the minds. The Chinese were the Chinese, and the Ocean-men were the Ocean-men. That was all there was to be said on either side as far as the Chinese were concerned. China being a world (not a world to itself, but actually the whole world), any one who lived in China was an inhabitant of the world and therefore a Chinese. Even the Ocean-men foreigners who came to live in China from some place as remote in the Chinese mind as the planet Mars had to have the privileges and burdens of Chinese because they were Chinese, in that they were inhabitants of the "World China."

The wonderful broadness of Confucianism had made the Chinese most liberal-minded toward all human beings; and this tolerance was further increased—and perhaps sweetened—by the affectionate teachings of the transplanted Buddhism. However, even this broad-minded attitude was overindulgent. It was so thinly expansive that it could only veil and not fully cover the needs of China. China, believing herself to be the whole world, put no value upon the elements of nationality. Why should one boast of being Chinese, when there was nothing else one could be? A Chinese was Chinese, because there was no other type of man save Chinese. There was no such thing as nationality among the Chinese, for they knew nothing of the other nations. Therefore, having no nationality, how could the Chinese have patriotism? Why was it, under this condition, that the fires of sectionalism in China at times burnt so fiercely? If there were no patriotism in China, what was it that inspired the boasting of the prowess of Chinese arms against the French? What was it that made the Chinese coolies boycott the contractors of French cruisers? It was not patriotism; it was racial coherence, and racial coherence and sectionalism were the very elements that overcame the development of Chinese patriotism. Racial coherence involved the observance of racial traditions and, under the Manchus, had even descended to the silly customs of wearing a queue.

It was during the Franco-Chinese War, while preaching reform, that Sun commenced to make a study of the Manchu troops. Concerning their numbers and equipment, he informed himself fully through every avenue of information. He learned that they did not use their guns with the skill of the French soldiers, and that they did not have that discipline which meant success with the rifle and the bayonet. The more he informed himself concerning the armed rule of the imperialists, the more vigorously (although in secret) he urged its overthrow.

## XXV

I DID not encumber the discussion of the early Hawaiian life of Wen with a statement which now becomes very important. Wen, at the time when he was ordered away from Honolulu by his brother Da Ko, was perhaps the wealthiest Chinese minor in the Hawaiian Islands. This wealth was his by reason of one of those peculiar partnerships which Chinese brothers frequently form, despite a great difference in age. Da Ko needed Wen in his shop and in his other businesses. He loved Wen and considered it fit to give him, in lieu of wages, a half-interest in his shop and other businesses. Da Ko had a lawyer prepare deeds to protect Wen in the security of his half of the holdings, which were constantly increasing in value with the development of Honolulu.

Da Ko had expected great things of Wen in the ancient Chinese way. He thought that some

184

day Wen would return to Blue Valley and use
his share of the communal fortune in some way
that would reflect credit upon every member of
the Sun family. Sad, indeed, was Da Ko when
he perceived that his younger brother was drift-
ing away from the models of correct Chinese
ancient life and was leaning toward the sadly
ruinous methods of the Ocean-men. He considered that there was only one way to try to redeem
Wen from the error of his foreign inclination,
and that was by commanding him to return immediately to Blue Valley, where, again under the
family influence, he would forget the ways of the
foreigner. I suppose that often when Da Ko
had started Wen safely back from Honolulu to
China, he would say complacently to himself:
"How glad I am that I have saved Wen from
those terrible foreign influences! Back home
they will teach him the good old Chinese ways,
and, together, we shall devote our fortune to honoring the whole family. How lucky it was that
I forecast all this, so that he sha'n't throw his
fortune away in dishonoring us by following the
foreign ways."

Alas, poor Da Ko! What a shock it must have
been to him when the message came from Blue
Valley telling him of Wen's madcap sacrileges,
culminating with his banishment because of his

185

mutilation of the village god. When Da Ko received this news he decided that a fortune would indeed be a dangerous thing for his younger brother to handle. He considered that it was his duty to regain possession of it at once. There was a great obstacle in the way, however. The title to this fortune was already in the name of Wen. In order to regain it, it would be necessary to have Wen come to Honolulu so that he could reconvey the properties to Da Ko. Da Ko, therefore, with feverish haste, sent out the message commanding Wen to come back to Honolulu.

Wen, prosecuting his studies at the English school at Hong Kong, was greatly surprised to receive the abrupt message asking him to return to the land from which he had been ordered away. He did not question the inconsistency, however, and immediately obtained his leave of absence from the school and started back on the first ship for Honolulu. Da Ko had commanded, and it was the duty of the younger brother to obey.

Wen found that the Hawaiian Islands had gone forward during the approximate two-year period of his absence. In two thousand years China had not improved itself as much as had the little Hawaiian Islands in that short period of two years.

Da Ko greeted him with the affection of old,

but the younger brother could see that there was a restraint and sadness in his greeting.

After the feast of welcome, Da Ko took Wen aside and sadly commented upon his waywardness, his disrespect for the time-honored Chinese customs, and the disgrace that he had brought upon the whole of the Sun family by his mutilation of the Northern Emperor. The Northern Emperor was held in great esteem by Da Ko, for it was the Northern Emperor that had guided him safely over the perilous sea and had finally brought him back to the land of his forebears with rich treasure.

"Wen, you will remember that I made over to you your half of our accumulations here in Hawaii," continued Da Ko. "Our prosperity is that of the whole family, but you have in your name half of what I have created here with your aid. When I made the deeds of the property over to you, I believed that you would follow the correct way of your ancestors. In this hope, however, I have been deceived sadly, for you persist in following the foreign ways and deride those customs which you should honor. Why, therefore, should you consider yourself entitled to half of these properties when its possession will prove your ruin in that you will waste this substance in stirring up trouble for yourself and

187

family? Our Chinese Government is good. If you continue to preach against it, the whole family will be despoiled and dishonored. With your foreign leanings you put yourself against our customs, our traditions, and all that we hold dear. This attitude may lead you eventually to separate yourself even from your family. Is it not just, then, that I take back that which so freely I have set aside for you?"

Wen was astonished at the words of his brother. He had given no thought to the past munificence of Da Ko. Wen had never known the pinch of poverty, although he knew what poverty itself was. Poverty was everywhere in China. Wen had gloried in Da Ko's success and did not consider that he had had a great part in its making. It was very wonderful to him that a Chinese, bound to the traditions of ancient precepts as was Da Ko, should be able to go forth in a strange *yan* (ocean) land, and there gain esteem and respect among foreigners by sheer business ability.

Wen in his astonishment remained silent, while Da Ko continued:

"It is good to come among the Ocean-men and labor with them. It is good to have their esteem. But if we lose the treasured traditions of China, if we do not follow the precepts of our ancestors, what happiness can come from a foreign-made fortune?"

"I am sorry if I have disappointed you," Wen finally confessed. "I am sorry that I cannot find my duty in the paths of the Chinese ancients. I would rather follow the way of the Chinese law than that of foreign law, should my conscience allow it. But China is not doing its duty to itself. I cannot conform to customs that break down rather than build up character. As for the property you have bestowed upon me so generously, I shall be glad to return it to you. I shall have no further claim to it. Great riches do not attract me. Money is one of the curses of China. Money has its uses and abuses, and unfortunately in China money and its corrupt use in official life put a burden on the people. Tell me, Brother, what I can do to restore the fortune to you, entire?"

Da Ko was overjoyed, for he had feared that the foreign teachings might have influenced Wen's character for the bad.

Da Ko lost no time in conducting Wen to a lawyer's office, where Wen signed back to Da Ko all his interest in the property Da Ko had made over to him.

Both brothers smiled when they left the lawyer's office and walked down through the busy lanes of Honolulu. Da Ko smiled because he

knew that if Wen still persisted in following the
mad ways of the foreigners, at least he would not
carry with him in his destruction half of the
fortune which had been so long and laboriously
gathered together.

Wen smiled because he was glad to do his
brother's bidding and because he had an opportunity to show again his love and devotion to Da
Ko, and moreover he felt that in the act of re-
nouncing the properties he had made a new com-
pact to work for the reform of China. He was
freer now to do as he wished. The family tie
was not broken but only loosened. Under the
new conditions that would prevail in the New
China toward which now his dreams were center-
ing, the family ties would again be tightened.
However, at the present time there was a parting
of the ways. His family would follow the contented path of ten thousand years, while he—he
did not exactly know.

Yes, for him—where lay the path? Now that
his last moment of decision had come and his
family were turning sorrowfully from him, things
were not as clear to him as they had been before.
No greater mishap can befall a Chinese than to
estrange himself from his family. Even in his
banishment from Blue Valley, his family had
stood by him; but now this act of renunciation in

the Hawaiian lawyer's office, did it not mean an
estrangement? Of his own volition he had taken
this fatal step. Where was the new path that he
must follow since he had resolved to turn away
from the old path of his forebears?

Alas, there was no path! He found that he
would have to blaze his own trail through the
wilderness of confusion that loomed up before
him, and, to add to his confusion, he had yielded
up that which might have meant success. Like
Jacob of old, Wen could have demanded of Da Ko
privileges and rights equal to that of the older
son, and Da Ko, like Esau of old, would have to
accede to his demand. Wen needed money for
his great plan to revolutionize China, needed it as
much as Esau needed the mess of red lentil pottage. Da Ko, like the famished hunter, returned
from the unsuccessful chase (the vague chase for
the ancient Chinese respect) and beheld the
hoarded wealth, as Esau beheld the mess of
pottage. However this savory dish of half a
fortune Wen yielded up without hesitation or
condition of price.

Instead of the vengeance sworn and the vows
to kill uttered in the mythical tale of the "shaggy
mountain land" of the past, these two brothers
parted with expressions of love and respect. One
had given all that he had of an elder brother's

counsel, and the other had given all that he had of wealth.

Surely the wrath of the painted but mutilated god of the temple of Blue Valley was appeased at last by this propitiation.

# FOURTH PERIOD

### 1886 to 1894
### Avocation and Vocation

## XXVI

CHOOSING A PROFESSION—CANTON MEDICAL COLLEGE
—HONG KONG MEDICAL SCHOOL—SUN'S DECLARA-
TION OF INDEPENDENCE—THE DARE-TO-DIES.

WHILE in Queen's College (academic) at Hong Kong, young Sun began to inform himself as to what profession in life he should follow in his purpose to work for the new China as soon as his academic education was completed. To do Reform work, he knew that he must have some professional vocation to start with, and perhaps for use as a cloak for his other work; for he felt that his eventual vocation would find itself in the dangerous field of revolution. When the revolution was started, then the vocation he had learned in the professional school would become his avocation.

Had there been an opportunity to go to a military school in China, he would have gone at once. This was denied him, as there was no military school in China; and he did not, of course, have any political support to get him admitted to foreign military schools. Manchu political strength was not given to Chinese students who were seeking to overthrow its dynasty.

He bethought himself of going to a naval college but the fulfilment of his desire in this regard was denied him by reason of the fact that in the Franco-Chinese War the French gunboats had destroyed Fuchow College, which was the only naval school China had.

He also considered becoming a lawyer; but there were no law-schools in China, the Chinese considering that they had no need for military or law schools. Hence, as a last choice of profession, young Sun turned to the profession of medicine and surgery, for through the Medical School of Hong Kong the way was open to him; and he also considered that the practice of medicine in China would lend itself easily to political intrigues, for doctors in China were considered politically innocuous. The Chinese practice of medicine (such as it was) was a free profession, open to all; any one had the right to hang out his sign as a healer. The proverbial good health of the Chinese caused them rarely to approach men who made a pretense of a knowledge of medicine. When a patient did seek medical advice, his disease or sickness had nearly always proceeded to its last stage, and hence there was only a faint hope that the acupuncture, plasters, or herbs offered could do any good. Modern surgery was practically unknown among the Chinese. Thus the native Chinese doctor was looked upon in a good-natured, tolerant way as half impostor and half successful necromancer. At all events, the Chinese tolerated the necromantic practice of medicine as innocuous and believed that if it did no good, at least, the sorcery did little harm. However, in becoming a modern surgeon, young Sun concluded that he could be of use in helping develop the real practice of medicine in China, as against the evils of the old-fashioned native practice. At the same time, this profession was to give him a cloak of security for the greater reform work in which he was to offer all that he had in life; yea, life itself!

Thus, having graduated first in his class from the Hong Kong Academic School, he entered the Pak Tsai Medical School in Canton. His primary, secondary, and academic education had, indeed, been thorough, and he was now well prepared for his professional studies. He selected the Canton Medical School, since it was an active center from which to develop the revolutionary work which he now planned somewhat more definitely. The teaching of this school was in Chinese, and the instructors were Americans.

He remained a year in the Canton Medical

School, concentrating his daytime efforts in the laboratory, the class and dissecting room, and the study chamber, so that certain hours should be free for his reform work. It was at this time that he formed his first revolutionary nucleus through the assistance of his classmate, Cheng Se Liang. It was also at this early period that he began the organization of the reform societies called Kao Lao Hwei, in which he originated three very useful forms of membership: military, civil, and patriotic contributory. From the military membership eventually were evolved the Dare-to-Dies.

In 1887 a new school of medicine and surgery was established at Hong Kong, and young Sun thought it would suit his revolutionary activities and his surgical study to change to that school. He remained in the Hong Kong Medical School for five years (from 1887 to 1892), and upon graduation in 1892 bethought himself of settling his revolutionary activity and medical practice in Macao. However, the Portuguese authorities made certain exactions of him, ostensibly in the matter of obtaining a license to practise, so that he concluded he would best return to Canton. Macao was a smaller city than either Hong Kong or Canton, and surveillance of his actions would therefore be easier. Hence, with the beginning of 1893 we find Dr. Sun with offices for the practice of medicine not only in the city of Canton itself but in one of its outskirts. This gave him two political rendezvous under cover of his professional work. He put in a surprising amount of time on his surgical cases (considering that his mind was more occupied with political matters), for he loved the practice of surgery, in which his reputation for skill had gone far and wide. On this account his practice, in spite of heavy charity work and political effort, was very lucrative.

Thus he continued his revolutionary labors under the professional guise of surgeon until 1895, when he was driven from China by imperial order, charged with complicity in the abortive effort of the Cantonese and Swatow revolutionists to make a joint attack against the Manchus. Space will not allow any detailed recital of the hard, painstaking effort put forth by Sun Yat Sen in his incipient revolutionary work from the time of his graduation from Hong Kong Medical College [1] in 1892 until his second thwarted attack in 1895 at Canton.

There are, however, two details in this period which it is essential to recall. The first of these

[1] This college is now merged in the University of Hong Kong, the name ''Hong Kong Medical School'' being the colloquial name generally used at that time.

is the formation of the Chinese Declaration of
Independence, which goes back even to this early
day; the other detail being the organization
Dare - to - Dies.

If any man deserves credit as the original sub-
scriber to the Chinese Declaration of Independence, that man is Sun Yat Sen. It was the per-
sistent cry of Sun's Declaration of Independence
that brought about the eventually successful
revolution that started at Wuchang in the Province of Hupeh on October 10, 1911.

This Chinese Declaration of Independence,
however, was not a document as with us; it was
not even a speech uttered in the dramatic way
that such declarations are presumed to be made.
Of course, the Chinese Declaration of Independence was at times written, and naturally it was
made a matter of discourse, particularly in the
conclaves of the secret fraternities organized by
Sun Yat Sen; but although it was not a formal
instrument such as one would imagine, it none
the less accomplished the effect that made our
own Liberty Bell ring.

Before Sun's activity, the idea of the overthrow of the Manchus was a vague and indefinite
continuation of the long-haired rebel opposition,
which, although intensely patriotic, did not make
up a formal logical protest that could serve as a

The only sure outlet the tens of thousands of hamlets such as this have is by the canal.

One of the unnumbered beauty-spots of a China that is a half-thousand miles from a railroad. On March 1, 1912, Sun resigned as President of China, to devote himself to modernizing China through railroads that would put new life into all the ancient corners such as the above.

A provincial tea-shop. "It was to the tea-shop that all Chinese went to get the news of the day" (Page 234).

Some of the more elaborate tea-shops have gardens such as this.

platform upon which to argue Chinese rights. No one before Sun had ever had the genius to conceive of a short-worded program that would awaken China to the need of reform. When we consider the very few political slogans which have ever been successful, we cannot but wonder at the success of Sun in inventing a slogan which was to awaken China out of its lethargy. It was this slogan, invented by Sun, which made up the Chinese Declaration of Independence that eventually overthrew the Manchus. It was a short declaration, containing in its original text only four Chinese words, but it hit the mark as nothing else could have done. Before giving these four words I think I should offer a word of explanation as to the way Sun invented the slogan.

Sun realized, when he came back from Honolulu in 1875 (his first return), that his success in any effort to overthrow the Manchus depended upon two things: his ability, first to keep his head on his shoulders and, secondly, to make a platform upon which he could stand. There was nothing before him from which he could make a platform. He could not find fault with the Son of Heaven, because the Son of Heaven was perfect, and no one had ever tried before to oppose him in a logical statement of fact. However, Sun, after casting his net around in the deep waters of his mind, pulled up an idea that, for a platform, was the simplest yet eventually the most winning slogan he could possibly have conceived. This platform or declaration was a protest, not against the Son of Heaven, but against reverence to his throne. If reverence to the throne could be overcome, then the Son of Heaven was without a job, for his patronage would be lost. It is unfortunate that the space of this volume will not allow a full explanation of what "reverence to the throne" meant to the subjects of the Son of Heaven. I do not think we have any equivalent of this sentiment in our combined Occidental history; for just as Chinese custom made filial obedience the first law of the family, so reverence to the throne was recognized as the first law of the race. Hence, when Sun first suggested, in the immunity of a secret order, an attempt to overthrow the great throne which Chinese custom had been taught to reverence, his lodge-fellows all asked, "What substitute would you then have for the throne?" Sun found it hard to give a satisfactory answer. If he replied, "Reverence for the law alone," the answer would be misunderstood. If he responded, "The sovereignty of the people," they could not understand because they did not know what the "sovereignty of the people" was. In fact, Sun's greatest difficulty consisted in knowing with just what words to begin his attack on the Son of Heaven. To the Chinese mind, the Son of Heaven was more than an emperor; he was more even than any chief ruler of our Occidental conception; for he was the direct representative of his subjects with the gods above. It was he alone, as the very highest priest of all, who went to pray for the whole nation at the Temple of Heaven. Every official of China might be corrupt, but it was not the fault of the Son of Heaven, for "he was benevolent, all his actions filled with grace, and he had the interests of the people dearer to his heart than his own blood."

Against all this, Sun Yat Sen finally evolved his declaration of four words,

*Tien Ming Wu Chang,*

which means,

Divine right does not last forever.

With this negative opening wedge, Sun gave the text of his opposition to reverence to the throne. There was nothing offensive to the masses in this simple, negative declaration, so adroitly conceived. Once he had the entering wedge driven into the sluggish minds of the people, he felt sure of the eventual victory. The most ignorant coolie could understand this simple and inoffensive, yet startling, slogan. In its

203

masterly composition Sun covered eventually the whole target of Chinese popular attention, finally enlarging it step by step until this Declaration of Independence may be translated, in its sense, about as follows:

> No longer shall we reverence the throne.
> The Son of Heaven is incompetent.
> His officers are corrupt.
> His rule is an abomination.
> He shall give way to the will of the people.
> No longer shall we reverence the throne.

\* \* \* \* \* \* \*

In addition to this detail of Sun's early revolutionary period, we should allow space to say something about his organization of the Dare-to-Dies. Without the Dare-to-Dies, Sun would have had no instrument with which to enforce his Declaration of Independence. Sun reasoned that as long as he was willing to die himself for this Declaration he could find others who would join him.

The Dare-to-Die originated from the lit-she. "Lit" means chevalier, knighthood, daring, and "she" is the masculine qualificative; hence the lit-she is the man who is willing to give his life for the welfare of others. In the mind of the Chinese, Christ was a lit-she. The doctrine of lit-she, applied to Chinese individual courage, produces a psychology that makes the Dare-to-Die.

The spirit of the Chinese battle mind is different from ours, for they have not gone so far as have we in separating all mob influence from military organization. All this involves a long discussion which we can obviate by dryly stating that the Chinese look to individual examples of courage more than we do. Perhaps I can explain what I mean by mentioning the following incident:

My editing headquarters in Chicago for the "Chinese Nationalist" adjoined a lodge-room of the Kuo Ming Tong, where there was displayed conspicuously a large picture of one of Sun's Dare-to-Dies who had been treacherously stabbed to death while he was asleep. I ordered the picture away from its conspicuous place, since it gave foreign visitors a sinister impression of the purpose of the movement, for the huge picture showed the Dare-to-Die with a great wound in his side, dead in his bed, just as he was found after his murder. The picture was cleverly done by a Chinese artist and horribly realistic, with a burnt-down candle beside the dead body to give the whole picture an emblematic touch.

Upon my order, the picture was immediately taken away, but, returning one day unexpectedly after a rather long absence, I found it in its old, conspicuous place; and with each of my irregular comings and goings, the painting, like a phantom, would likewise come and go. This was during the period of the Punish-Yuan Expedition, when certain of the Dare-to-Dies were returning to China from abroad.

Upon my final remonstrance, one of the members said to me apologetically:

"Excuse us, please, if we like to have it there. It *cheers us up so.*"

This explanation came so ingenuously that I could not restrain my suddenly evoked amusement, and although I myself could find nothing in the horribly lifelike picture of a murdered and bleeding body to cheer me up, I remonstrated no longer, for I realized that this terrible portrayal of the death of one of their leaders ever held out to them an example of the courage demanded of a Dare-to-Die in that way so different from ours.

"How does a Dare-to-Die look?" some one may ask. I think I am rather disqualified to say much concerning the Dare-to-Dies, by reason of my immeasurable admiration for them; an admiration that at times, in individual, and even humble, cases, amounted almost to a feeling akin to hero-worship. Among these humble heroes was the untutored cook mentioned in the preface of this volume. So I should say that to me, at least, a Dare-to-Die always looks his part. There is a certain expression that I think I find on their faces that I can recognize anywhere: a clear, open look right out into the world, and a smile of fortitude that speaks of martyrdom. There is no sense of amusement in this smile. It is not the smile that breaks into a laugh, nor the sneering smile of a fanatic. It is a smile of anticipation, as though waiting for that supreme moment to come when the full purpose of life is to be realized dramatically in its purposeful and unflinching surrender. Perhaps I might liken it to the smile of a child that in time of danger stands by the side of its parent, believing that all is well. The Dare-to-Die must be cheerful, and he must be courageous. This smile of friendly cheer and courage is his badge of temperament.

And with this smile the Dare-to-Die goes to the torture-rack, faces the firing-squad, engages in the bloodiest hand-to-hand conflict, takes the cold cut of the bayonet or the red spit of the gun without flinching, without regret.

For lack of space I shall desist, however, from the loquacity I feel in recalling memories of the Dare-to-Dies, reserving for the chapter entitled, "Sun and Hwang Hsing," something further in this regard.

# FIFTH PERIOD

## 1895 to October 11, 1896
### First Fugitive Period

This period covers the time from Sun Yat Sen's second thwarted attack at Canton in 1895 to October 11, 1896, when he was kidnapped by the Chinese Legation at London.

## XXVII

### THE FIRST PRICE ON SUN'S HEAD

I SHALL simmer this period down to a skeleton chapter.

While Sun Yat Sen was using the instrument of his profession to advance the purposes of his political aim, he had secret organizations established at Hong Kong, at Macao, and particularly at Canton. His fame went abroad as one skilled in the art of healing, and there was no suspicion attached to his labor. It was a rare opportunity which he guarded most jealously, expecting every day that it would come to an end. However, Providence favored Sun Yat Sen in giving him over two years in which to go about unmolested, laying the corner-stone of his great political enterprise.

In 1894 the Chino-Japanese War broke out. Sun made a quick trip to Hawaii and then on to the United States, in order to secure the funds necessary to make the first attack. By his eloquence he overcame the incredulity of the liberty-loving Chinese, asserting that the war with the Japanese

211

would give the patriots their first chance for an entering wedge. He, however, was disappointed in obtaining the revolutionary funds needed, although among the followers he obtained on this voyage there were two who gave up their entire wealth for the first revolutionary attack. Sun's plan was to seize the yamen at Canton and use it as a base of further operations. In the chapter entitled, "Sun and Hwang Hsing," we shall speak further of this yamen, which for many years was the first goal aimed at by Sun.

Sun had organized at Hong Kong a sort of trading concern under which to cover his activity there, and had also established an ostensible agricultural society in Canton, likewise to cover his movements. With the funds which Sun had collected, dollar by dollar, he bought a great quantity of high-grade, small firearms, among these munitions being six hundred revolvers, with which it was expected that the Dare-to-Dies would be able to make the first onslaught against the yamen. However, by some treachery that even the precaution of Sun could not circumvent, these very essential six hundred revolvers were seized by the Manchu authorities, and some of the brave Dare-to-Dies upon whom Sun had counted were put to death. Nevertheless, the onslaught was carried out against the yamen during the ninth

moon of 1895, but, because of the lack of the six
hundred revolvers for the Dare-to-Dies, the whole
effort resulted in a gloomy and disheartening
failure. The Manchus put a price upon Sun's
head, and after great difficulties he managed to
escape, finally finding his way back to Hawaii.
Here, undaunted by his recent failure, he proceeded cheerfully to renewed activity in political
organization. Considering the bloody defeat of
his first effort of the ninth moon, 1895, it is
strange to consider that at Hawaii he actually
met with more success than previously. From
Hawaii he went on to America, where, likewise,
he met with some success, then proceeding to the
Continent of Europe, where we find him on the
very eventful day of October 11, 1896. It was on
this day that he was kidnapped by the Chinese
Legation at London, to which reference is unnecessary here, since the details are given from
first-hand sources in the most interesting book
published in 1914 by Dr. James Cantlie, entitled,
"Sun Yat Sen and the Awakening of China." I
have never had the pleasure of meeting Dr.
Cantlie, but I hereby express my deep admiration
of him for having saved Sun Yat Sen from the
Manchu authorities in London. I understand
that Dr. Cantlie, by reason of other services to
humanity, has been knighted; and, judging merely

from his attitude toward the Chinese, the honor was, indeed, most highly merited.

The kidnapping episode made Sun Yat Sen's name very generally known throughout the English-speaking world. I believe that Sun Yat Sen would have been in a better position for his political work had he not had all the publicity attendant upon the attempt of the Manchus to destroy him. His revolutionary work had to be done among the Chinese almost exclusively. The publicity increased him in importance more among his enemies than among his followers, and hence was perhaps more of a disadvantage than an advantage to him.

# SIXTH PERIOD

## October 11, 1896, to December 6, 1911
### INTENSIVE REVOLUTIONARY METHODS

In this period Sun becomes more certain of his success because he has found the methods which are the best instruments for revolutionary work.

## XXVIII

### NO. 121, UNDER THE HILLSIDE

FIRST of all, I think we should consider that
Sun Yat Sen founded the Chinese Republic
by the method of sheer fearlessness. Sun does
not know what fear is. His courage is both
physical and moral, and both sorts are dominated
by his intelligence, much as the range-finder
elevates or depresses the field-piece, according to
the range.

If it is a small danger, then Sun will use up
none of the ammunition of his bravery whatsoever but, in his quiet Chinese fashion, simply slide
out of the way. If the peril is great, so much the
greater becomes his courage. One of his followers
once said to me, "Never was a gun made quick
enough to get Sun, for his lightning-like adaptation to circumstances is as quick as the explosion
of a shell." Allowing for the hero-worship involved in this remark, as a metaphor its application is useful.

Perhaps I may best indicate this fearless

quality of Sun by relating the incidents of his coming to have dinner with us one night back in 1919 in Shanghai. In that busy period we lived in a great ramshackle building in a district of Shanghai out beyond Hongkew, called Chappei. To get to Chappei one had to pass through Shanghai's underworld district known as the Trenches, which attracted dissolute and desperate characters of both sexes from every nation under the sun. Brawls were almost hourly occurrences and murders not infrequent. Around the Trenches with its gaudy ball-rooms, bars, and bawdy-houses there was a bad Chinese district where many evil-doers found hiding-places.

It was at a rather disturbed time (July, 1919), an ex-governor of an adjoining province having been gunned to death but a few days before. Shortly before the hour set for the coming of Dr. Sun and his wife, I reflected upon the dangers of the neighborhood that lay between us and the Bund, the Bund being the main business and maritime thoroughfare of Shanghai. Finally I imparted something of my fears to my wife, and she, in her turn, became apprehensive as to the safety of Dr. Sun.

We both concluded that it would not be prudent for the doctor to come up by the Szechuen Road, which went through the heart of the Trenches,

218

and so I went to the telephone with the intention of changing the place of dinner from our home to a private dining-room of the Astor House Hotel. I was informed, however, that he had left his home and was already on his way with Mrs. Sun. In a rather guilty and panic-stricken condition, we waited.

Then the rattle of carriage-wheels sounded through the little park that surrounded the great lonely house, and there the Suns appeared in an open horse-drawn vehicle. The doctor was dressed in a white linen gown and looked a very big target both for observation and ammunition.

We imparted none of our fears to the Suns during the whole delightful evening until at its very close, when I suggested in as offhanded a manner as I could assume:

"Doctor, let me send Mrs. Sun and you home in a closed motorcar."

"No, I thank you; the night is hot, and we enjoy greatly the open carriage."

I saw the difficulty, and so I took Sun to one side and frankly imparted my fears to him: how he would have to return through a very dangerous quarter, how his enemies might be more active than he suspected, how that very morning I had appeared in court on behalf of the widow of an ex-governor, who had been foully murdered

219

while riding in a rickshaw, a fusillade of bullets riddling him and the vehicle.

Sun followed my expression of fears with a look of amusement that grew with the recital of my apprehensions; then he laughed one of his quiet little laughs, as if I had told him a funny tale.

"Nonsense!" he finally declared. "There is no danger."

Again I urged that he let me send him and his wife home in a closed car. I spoke of the lateness of the hour, the poorly lighted condition of Szechuen Road, and its darkened labyrinth of alleys just before it wound through the Trenches. All in vain. In an undisturbed and happy mood he gave the order for his carriage, and after a rather long and lingering conversation in the garden and at the edge of the compound he drove away, still with something of amusement showing on his face as he waved good-by. How relieved we were when, after great suspense, we found that the Suns had safely arrived home after the long four-mile drive!

I hope this little incident will give something of an idea of the absolute fearlessness of Sun Yat Sen, and that it will enable the reader better to understand Sun's almost mad disregard for danger during the long period when he operated

220

his revolutionary control, particularly at No. 121, Under the Hillside.

We are speaking of Sun's methods in this period, and in connection with his fearlessness I should mention that frequently this fearlessness is passive. In fact, many of Sun's methods are passive. We have seen that even his first enunciated Declaration of Chinese Independence was negative. In this passivity Sun is not without great and lasting precedents. Even the ancient school of Chinese wrestlers made wrestling the art of throwing the adversary by means of his own strength.

"Make the strength of your enemy prove his undoing. Consider yourself as the leverage to break his bones, as soon as he shall waste enough strength upon you. Do not resist your adversary. Let him apply his whole strength upon you. Then, by an adroit passivity, let him crack his bones on the obstacle of your own change of balance. His force is the sledge-hammer; your force is the anvil. Your adversary breaks himself between his hammer and your anvil."

This wrestler's method may be taken as something of a summary of Sun's political wrestling. Sun's tactics throughout the whole thirty years of his revolutionary work have been those of a political wrestler following the ancient Chinese school, to whose passivity and patience he added his supreme courage. He knew these to be the only methods that would succeed, for he, in support, was weak, his adversary strong. Sun was clever and agile; the imperial colossus was stupid and over-muscled. Sun was clear-headed; the Manchu giant saw dimly the smaller things before him. Sun shifted his defense as swiftly and easily as the flight of the eagle; things trembled with his enemy's slightest movement. At first it seemed like a fly fighting an elephant; but just as the drop of water opens up the way for the deluge, so Sun wrestled along in the farthest shadow of the colossal bulk of his imperial enemy, pounding into the huge carcass whatever he could of destruction, now advancing, now retreating; getting nearer and nearer for that eventual master-blow that was to make the Lilliputian the master of the giant. It was a terrific struggle for thirty years, with the odds so unequal that any one who does not know Sun personally might wonder how it could have ever happened.

For simple as the old jiu-jitsu instructions are, the wrestling method does not work out in practice as announced in theory, unless there is a mental and physical superiority on the one side not possessed by the other. In Sun's case the superiority consisted in being a genius.

This political jiu-jitsu method was really the only scheme upon which Sun could have won. The dribble of funds cheerfully given him by patriotic Chinese never remained in his hands long enough even to accumulate into a substantial pool. Sun really never had enough cash money in those whole thirty years of struggle (excepting, of course, the close-up campaign) even to put into China from overseas one fully equipped regiment for each of the branches of the war service. Revolutions and rebellions have been popular in South and Central America because of the ease with which *coups d' état* could be executed. Sun realized from the very beginning that a Chinese *coup d' état* could not be realized in the European sense. Again, revolutions have been frequent, both in Europe and America, because of the ease with which economic support could be found for political change; but Sun had none of these advantages.

Our digression has now brought us to a point in Sun's life when for him all was at a very low ebb, the summer of 1899, when he sought refuge in Japan from the imperial orders against him.

To avoid confusing this sojourn with others in Japan, let us bear in mind the following: In 1885 Sun, then nineteen years old, passed through the seaports of Japan on his first return from Honolulu; in 1895 he was a refugee in Japan, where as previously noted he cut off his queue to aid his disguise; in 1899, extraterritoriality being abolished, he established his headquarters at Yokohama to try to bring the revolutionary movement back to life.

In this summer of 1899, an ordinary man—yes, a very superior man—would have said to himself:

"I think that I have had enough of revolution against the Manchus. I shan't surrender, but I shall slip away to some quiet, neutral spot abroad, where I can practise my profession and have something of the ease and comfort of life. I have done the best I could. Now let some other leader come forward to carry on the good work, for verily I have done my share, and the rewards are still as remote as the end of an unknown journey. I have been working for a dozen years on a program that gets nowhere. Many of my followers have been tortured and imprisoned, and many have been executed, and now the friends and relatives of these brave men look upon me as a visionary, who can never accomplish what he has set out to do. All the money I have been receiving has brought us no actual triumph. Imperial Peking is as defiant as ever, with added prices on my head. Fighting an empire is not a one-

Dr. Sun (seated) during the "No. 121 Hillside" sojourn in Japan
(Page 217).

Dr. Sun (in right-hand corner) at Yokohama in 1899.

man affair; so now let some one else carry on the
fight where I leave off.''

It was not in Sun's nature to say anything of
the sort, but the facts are that he was at this
time of seeking refuge in Japan in the summer
of 1899, just about as near a complete failure as
a man can go without tumbling to pieces. Had he
at this time fallen sick, or if the activity of his
enemies had prevented him coming in close contact with his following, it would not have been
surprising if Sun had been put so far back in his
labor as to leave the Manchu, even to the present
day, upon the Peacock Throne.

— However, in this low-tide period of revolutionary intensity, although Sun realized that he was
sliding down the ladder, at the same time he considered that he was gaining greater strength for
the climb back. He knew that the efforts of his
enemies had been redoubled against him, but the
years of failure and discouragement only screwed
his courage up to a higher point. The lower he
went in the hopes of his followers, the higher he
raised that point of success which he eventually
expected to reach.

So in his predicament at this most discouraging
period, Sun, in his usual way, did a very superb
thing; he went back as a refugee to Japan and
made his headquarters at Number One Twenty-

one, under the Hillside, a headquarters which will be explained shortly.

Japan was to Sun a very providential refuge in those early years of tribulation. With all the other approaches to China closed to him, this far-away point could still be used as headquarters to direct the attacks against the Manchus. Sun went to Japan more frequently than is mentioned in these sketches, and sometimes almost clandestinely; for in Japan he was not only sure of the support, sympathy, and protection of the several thousand Chinese merchants who lived in the Japanese port towns but, indeed, likewise of the friendship of certain Japanese friends, who thoroughly sympathized with his movement.

And now let us find out what "121, Under the Hillside," means.

Those of you who have been in Yokohama will remember the Bluff, where there were a number of pretty foreign residences and some of the consulates. A tide-water canal flowed at the foot of this Bluff, and on the other side of the canal stood the Grand Hotel. A street ran down between the canal and the hotel, and if you followed this street toward the triangle of a brick building (where a French baker served a wonderful *table d' hôte* for foreigners) you would have found in the next block a foreign-style wood, tile, and

226

plaster house known and numbered as One Twenty-one Yamashita Cho. *Yama* in Japanese means hill, *shita* means below, and *cho* means district; so this house was literally "House No. 121, Under-the-Hill District." The Yamashita, among the Japanese, was looked upon curiously, for it was there that all foreigners were compelled to live, in order that the Japanese authorities might check up on them when they desired.

When in July, 1899, extraterritoriality was abolished in Japan, Sun saw an opportunity to show an added defiance to his great and powerful imperial enemy, and conceived a plan which, for sheer political audacity, excites our admiration. He made up his mind in this hour of his extremity to set up his business of revolution under the very nose of the Manchus. Taking the location of the imperial consulate at Yokohama as the basis of his strategy, he leased the very nearest available house he could find, in which to install the new headquarters of his movement, and thus throw down the gantlet of challenge to his enemy at arm's length. This house was known and numbered as 121, Under the Hillside.

If Sun could have obtained the house next door to the imperial consulate he would have done so, but as it was he got near enough to the consular domicile and flag of the Middle Kingdom to watch every movement made and thus reiterate his challenge against his enemy every hour of the day. But at that, he played the game squarely with his adversary, for since the Manchu consulate was straight through the block from Sun's headquarters the Imperialists had the opportunity of picking Sun off with shot-gun or rifle every time he came or went. This taunting audacity was a bitter pill for the Manchus, for taking Sun's life would have caused a murderous wholesale reprisal against all the members of the Manchu consular staff; and letting him remain in defiance at their very door meant an acknowledgment of his strength as against their weakness.

In spite of prophesies to the contrary, Sun stayed on at 121, Under the Hillside. His movement took on new life, from the moment when he thus joined the issue.

Before the abolition of extraterritoriality the imperial consulate, just through the block, could have tried Sun one hour and strangled him in a cellar the next. With extraterritoriality abolished, and confident of reprisals in the event his life were taken, Sun blithely came and went in spite of the higher and higher prices placed on his head. There is a racy humor in this situation that those of us who think we understand something of Chinese character will readily appreciate. It was carrying the Chinese game of "cheek" to the fullest strategic victory. Again the nimble-minded Lilliputian outwitted the clumsy colossus. Nor was this "sit-in" game without something of excitement, for rumors were continually circulating through the settlement as to what action against Sun would be murderously taken by the Manchus.

Finally, in view of an extra added price put on Sun's head, it was thought that, in spite of fear of reprisals, Sun's obsequies were the order of a near day. A great many people continually were coming and going from Sun's headquarters, and because of Sun's accessibility his demise was deemed only the matter of a few weeks. Whether it would be by bomb, knife, two-edged sword, or pistol was a matter of occasional street gossip. Street gossip also had it that Sun was constantly shadowed and protected by a great prize-fighter from the Loochoo Islands. The Japanese have a high regard for the big hulking strappers from the Loochoo Islands, perhaps because after the Loochoo Islanders had paid tribute to both China and Japan for many years they were finally induced to forsake China for Japan and thereby gain strong favor among the Japanese, who attribute great courage and other qualities to these big natives from the far-away sea, south of Formosa.

According to the gossip of the street, this giant Loochoo body-guard was the ever-vigilant instrument that protected Sun from assassination.

I was much interested in the story of the Loochoo sleuth and prize-fighter, which I obtained (as well as the other information in this chapter) from local Yokohama sources; so one day I said to Sun, "I am much interested in the street gossip concerning the Loochoo body-guard in Yokohama back in '99."

Sun's puzzled look was the answer, and it subsequently developed that street gossip had taken one of Sun's faithful Cantonese followers for a Loochoo Islander. Sun the Unafraid has no need of body-guard.

But if the Under-the-Hillside district was interested in Sun, Sun had no time to be interested in it; this was the great "make-good" period of Sun's life, and he treasured every hour for building up his following. He realized the value of the confidence that his following had placed in him, and likewise realized that he had little to show in a tangible way for their confidence and for the treasure that had been given him from all parts of the world. As we have before mentioned,

230

with the contributions he had received Sun had made no substantial headway. He had purchased arms, and traitors had prevented their delivery to the revolutionary bands. To assure delivery, he himself had supervised the shipment of arms under the very noses of the Imperialists, only to find that fate again was against him, and the arms were seized. For all the money received he had little to show other than his own unabated enthusiasm. Now, in 1899, almost at the end of his rope, in the shadow of the Manchu consulate he worked strenuously to put more of the breath of life into the revolutionary movement, which was still regarded as visionary by all save Sun and his followers.

From all parts of the world these followers would come to visit him. There was even something in Japan itself of his following. There were about twenty-five hundred Chinese merchants or employees in Yokohama, most of whom were Cantonese. All these, almost to a man, were won over to Sun's support by the force of his leadership. There were also Chinese in Nagasaki, and although they were mostly Ningpo men, they were also with Sun, as were also the Foochow Chinese in Kobe and Osaka.

Sun, however, seems to regard this period as one neither of discouragement or danger. It was the gather-together period of the revolution, in which Sun renewed his efforts with added intensity.

"Did you not become discouraged, Doctor, after so many years of waiting?"

"If a man starts building a house, is he discouraged if he has to wait for materials? We never waited for labor; we only waited for materials."

Hence, during this period of waiting for material, he found that this taunt, this bravado, if you will, this challenge, uttered daily with all the sublimity of its audacity against the Manchus from No. 121, Under the Hillside, was a great means for reviving a cause weakened by repeated failures. Such conduct shows the versatility of Sun. It was only by the use of such dramatic schemings that he was enabled to keep the machine of his revolution in operation.

In after years, No 121, Under the Hillside, became a spot held in great respect among Sun's followers. Steps were taken to purchase the building and turn it into a memorial of Sun's work in Japan. While these efforts were in progress, the dreadful earthquake of September 1, 1923, came. The house was thrown down at the first shock, and its débris utterly demolished by fire.

## NO. 121, UNDER THE HILLSIDE

Sun's home and headquarters at Yokohama are gone forever, but the spirit of the Republic that he finally founded still soars onward.

On one of those great monuments which posterity shall some day erect to Sun Yat Sen, I hope that they will carve just these words:

1899–1900
No. 121, Under the Hillside.
No fear, no discouragement:
A dozen years of failure:
But the Day of Glory shall come.

## XXIX

### FROM TEA-HOUSE TO SECRET LODGE—SUN
### AND THE WORKING-MAN

THE MANCHU idea was to have the people under a control that would at any time allow an investigation into what any person thought, so far as his open speech indicated. The tea-shop was therefore favored by Manchu authority since it was a meeting-place easily controlled. Meetings for the open discussion were prohibited, but the tea-house open to the public was an institution where every one's expression could be kept under the surveillance of authority with convenience and certainty.

The main reason why the Chinese Republic has not gone forward more rapidly is that the Chinese are not accustomed to public expression in political matters, and it was only upon the publication of a book of Rules of Order for Public Speaking by Sun Yat Sen that the Chinese secured a basis for the discussion of public matters.

The tea-shop in China has from time immemorial been the center of all the gossip of the villages and the city. It was to the tea-shop that all Chinese went to get the news of the day. The tea-shop was both his morning and his evening paper. Most of the practical education of his life, outside of his own craft or vocation or trade, came from the gossip that was uttered by the oracles of the tea-houses.

Now, drinking tea is a very harmless pastime. The tea-houses are not immoral places. Chinese do not gamble to a very great extent in tea-houses, and there are, as a rule, no immoral women allowed in them. The tea-houses are merely gossip-places for idlers, who, as a part of the whole program of idling, buy a pot of tea for a couple of coppers. The highest price ordinarily charged for tea is six coppers,[1] and hence it would be unjust to condemn the tea-houses; they are not money-wasters, and, by comparison with the old whisky bars of the Occident, they are places of Sunday-school entertainment. To give an idea of their innocuousness, let us try to portray a tea-house habitué.

Down along the quiet side street of a Chinese city, where the great walls lead out into the country, just note the grotesque figure in a big farmer's apron and gown. In one hand he car-

[1] About two American cents, in November, 1924.

235

ries a tea-pot and in the other a little leather sack of tea. He is a near-by farmer whose little plot of ground may be seen from the walls of the city. He is dressed with comfort, wearing stockings and shoes, although his whole attire shows something of the need of renewal. He is a man of middle age and has an intensely distracted look on his face as he goes forward dangling his tea-pot and his tea-sack in his hands. He is going to the tea-house for his regular afternoon tea. He has worked hard from the dark hours of the early morning. Now, after his frugal mid-afternoon meal, he is on his way to the tea-shop. He carries his own kettle and his own tea, because with these accessories he will only have to spend one copper for the hot water, while he sits in the tea-house through a part of the afternoon and gets all the news. News is as essential to the human soul as drink or food to the human body. Even savages must have their news; the Chinese, with their highly developed ancient civilization, are no exception to the rule that a man to be really human must know what is going on in the world. Hence, the farmer lays his labor aside for an hour or so every day in order to go to town and get the news. This excursion is not only a pleasure to him; it is his right. What is it that the farmer will get at the tea-house? Just about

236

the same gossip that is set forth in a modern
newspaper adapted to ancient Chinese civilization. In the first place, he will want to know what
his products are selling for. Then there will be
local gossip. Wang will have sold ten *mows*
of land to Wong at fifty taels a *mow*. There will
be a new addition built upon the godown (or
warehouse) of Ching. Small items such as these
make up the substance of commercial and agricultural tea-shop gossip.

What objection is there to this? Why should
any one decry the innocent enjoyment of gossip-
ing and drinking tea? Merely because the tea-
shop has become for the Chinese headquarters
for idleness. Around the tea-house centers a
group of loafers ready to accept any statement a
member of the gentry makes. With a receptive
audience of idlers, any propaganda that does not
disturb ancient standards is acceptable. These
loafers are not loafers by natural inclination, for
the instinct of industry among the Chinese is too
active to develop loafing as a national character-
istic. The Chinese loafers, aside from this small
percentage of tea-house heroes, are loafers by
necessity rather than by choice. They loaf because they find no work; the lack of work is one
of China's greatest misfortunes. The tea-shop
in China has from time immemorial been an

adjunct to every household among Chinese city dwellers, so far as the male members of the family are concerned, and the influence of their enforced idleness has shown little effect upon them in spite of the tea-house heroes.

Sun realized early that he could work no political reform through the tea-house. As against tea-house idleness, Sun offered the secret fraternity. Lodges are everywhere attractive the world over. Every man is, by nature, a "joiner"; and in Sun's lively fraternal lodges there was the charm of secrecy that brought nightly increases in membership. Even the poorest Chinese, if he were decent and self-respecting and otherwise acceptable, could join a lodge; needless to say, he had his tea in the lodge under better conditions than he had it in the sloppy tea-house.

Sun made the foundation of his political movements sure and solid when he turned from the tea-house and formed the lodge out of whatever material was available.

And now a few words concerning Sun and the working-man, for his secret lodges took in the working-man along with Chinese of other grades.

I have, at times, been somewhat exasperated by the disparaging tone which I have so often heard in the voices of ax-to-grind foreigners living in China, who end up their criticism of Sun Yat Sen with something like this:

"Well, I suppose that Sun is all right with the Chinese laboring classes, for they all seem to follow him. But how can a man reform China through Chinese laborers?"

There is just enough point to this declaration to require more explanation than the limit of this sketch will allow. However, suffice it to say that Sun Yat Sen does stand for the working-man, and by working-man is meant every man who makes an honest living at manual labor. Sun stands for the Chinese working-man just as he stands for the Chinese farmers; because they make up the great majority of the Chinese racial representation and are the classes that suffered the most severely under Manchu tyranny. But he does not stand for these great Chinese classes to the detriment of the merchant or of the commercial or industrial classes. Sun stands for all China as represented in its new democracy; incidentally Chinese workmen and farmers form the foundation of the new Republic.

The allegation that Sun is a "working-man's leader" arraigns against him much of foreign capitalism, which thus looks upon him at times as inimical to its interests, in that he can encourage Chinese labor to ask for continued advances in wages. To those of us who know Sun, such an idea is entirely untenable, for Sun's conception of reform takes in the whole Chinese race. Sun is not a labor agitator. His following had always been made up very largely of men of some education and of family association who have ofttimes more than average pecuniary independence. His following of course comprises patriotic Chinese of all conditions, and it has included large numbers who represent the Chinese arts and crafts; in other words, the workingmen.

Perhaps the idea that Sun is, so to speak, a working-man's candidate for popular favor may come from the fact that during the many years of his revolutionary work the literary class of China, as aspirants for Manchu favors, did not in any great degree openly encourage his reform efforts. Again, perhaps the idea has come from Sun's unswerving honesty and simple mode of life, for he himself leads a straight-away, wholesome, hard-worked existence that might, by some, be likened to that of the man toiling for his bread in the sweat of his brow.

I have endeavored to show from the foregoing that Sun Yat Sen produced much of his revolutionary force by changing the idle energy of the

Pirates' heads hung in crates from the walls of the city.

A commonplace acrobatic stunt, in which the under acrobat is as
complacent as the one standing on his head. When such scenes
as the above attract but small attendance or observation, does
it not seem wonderful that Dr. Sun was able eventually to get
the masses interested in his revolutions?

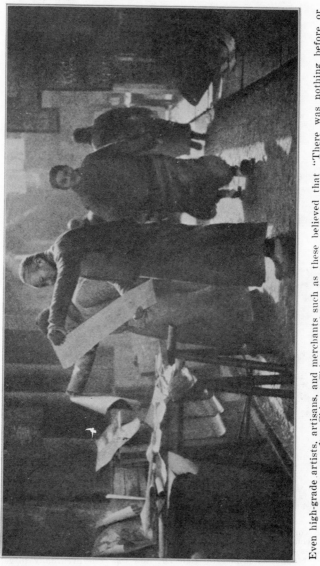

Even high-grade artists, artisans, and merchants such as these believed that "There was nothing before or after China. China was the beginning and the end" (Page 180).

tea-shop into the active force of the lodge-room, where even the hard-worked artisan had his welcome place. Sun never could have attained high success as a revolutionist except through this method, for all other methods were too expensive. It is remarkable how little money was ever used by Sun for actual propaganda work. The money went for guns and ammunition, for the use of volunteers who had graduated from the tea-shop in large numbers to become ardent lodge adherents, and who united with the great army of the working-men.

One day I asked Sun:

"Doctor, how much further do you think that you would have driven your reform to-day if you had had, well, say, Napoleon's treasury?"

Sun did not appear surprised at the question, and replied in a rather offhand manner:

"Money does not always work out. Peking has had a great treasure to expend, and still it has gained no real friends. Money is the lesser essential in reform, once the people are awakened to their rights."

One of the greatest financial successes of Sun was in 1910 when he raised fifty thousand dollars for the purchase of munitions for the Dare-to-Dies. We read in the inventory of Napoleon's wardrobe that his grand fur mantle of seventy-six pieces of ermine cost, with its gold embroideries, its linings and accessories, about the equivalent of this sum, taking the comparative value of money at the respective times into consideration.

With a comparison such as this in mind, we can, indeed, believe that "money is the lesser essential." I did not ask Sun what the other essential was, for any one who knows Sun would find the answer in a word that spells out on the fingers of the right hand "loyal," and on the fingers of the left hand, "faith."

"Money, the lesser essential." Essential, yes, but secondary to the element of loyalty as between leader and followers, with faith as the polar star before them. It was in the depths of the soul that this loyalty, this faith, empty-handed of silver or gold, conjured up that Angel of Wrath, Sun's Army of the People, to which, in 1911, his first proclamation was:

"Other revolutions have been made for the benefit of a hero. To-day it is a revolution of all the citizens."

I cannot resist the temptation to digress here, in order to show Sun's faith and loyalty for the people, to mention an incident at the abdication ceremonies of the Manchu Imperial Throne at Peking in 1911. Sun, as the representative of the people, purposely had the ceremony set in the upper story of the palace. Establishing himself there first, he literally made the Imperial Throne climb up to the people as represented by him.

Although Sun succeeded, through a program of self-suppressed, secret, and unostentatious progress, I think that foreigners would like him better to-day if he assumed something of the dazzling magnificence of the old Peacock Throne. It has been, and still is, in his power so to do; for there is practically no limit to the treasure in money and property of which Sun can possess himself, for his own personal use, if he so wishes. Foreigners do not like *poor* reformers, and that is just what Sun was, and still is to-day; a man with a moral purpose greater, to him, than all the wealth of the old Middle Kingdom.

There is another reason why Sun, unlike his enemies either in Peking or among the *tuchuns,* puts duty to the people higher than personal wealth. Sun is one of those rare geniuses of leadership who can hold command even when they have descended from the high seat of authority. Sun needs no throne or lofty chancel from which to exercise his control. Sun, the Founder of the Chinese Republic, stands down among men.

243

## XXX

IN THIS period of Sun's life we are dealing with his revolutionary methods. Our discussion would be incomplete if we did not speak of his active methods of campaigning, which are so sharply in contrast with his passive method of silence and watchfulness. Before speaking of his oratory, a few words in regard to his personal appearance.

Something above average height, supple of shoulder and quick of limb, erect, brow held high, Sun rather seems to belong to the military than to the civil side of life. The hard years of child labor in the Blue Valley of his birth still show in his power and quickness of muscle. His visage is boldly formed with prominent features, his nose being rather large for a Chinese with, at times, something of dilation in the fine nostrils. His forehead is high and lofty and of unusual breadth; his cheek-bones are not so prominent as one expects to see them among the Chinese; and the slant to the eyelids is almost impercep-

244

tible. His features are cast in a heroic mold but lighted up with a gentleness of manner which, at times, is almost womanly in its expression. There is a magnetic hold about his demeanor that makes men say of him, "Here is a man you can trust." One day I took a prominent foreigner over to call on him, and after leaving the house the caller repeated, as in an abstraction: "Oh, what wonderful eyes! He looks right through you!" Sun does, indeed, have a most magnetic gaze, particularly when his eyes kindle up in a great glow and stare out like a lion. His eyes are perfectly focused, clear, far-seeing, and penetrating; not with an inquisitive penetration, but with the wide range depth of the king of the jungle as he takes in at a glance the whole stretch of the mountain.

And, strange to relate, this man of great activity has the power of absolute relaxation. During those long, pleasant days we were together, I often wondered at his ability to remain still, for he would sit without a movement of the muscles, in an easy, graceful posture that belonged rather to an artist's studio than to a hot library on a steaming Shanghai summer day. His voice is low and gentle, his emphasis coming rather from his eyes than from his voice, but every phrase carried through like the tick of a metronome, clean to the end, with the push of the brain behind every word. I have rarely known him to repeat a word or to hesitate in its enunciation. Even over the telephone his voice comes sustained and gentle, but clear as a bell.

Sun is what some people would call a quiet man. Once at a reception I looked for him everywhere. He was the principal guest. Finally I found him in a retired corner, looking over the throng of uniforms and formal dress. He had escaped and found his refuge in that quiet nook and was merely looking at the throng. I, too, for a long time, and even after many days passed with him, thought that Sun was a quiet man. Then one night I heard him make a speech.

The corridor and street before the building were jammed with Chinese and foreigners; so I took my little boy upon my shoulder, and, through the courtesy of the student crowd, we made our way slowly to the main entrance. I was astounded at what I saw before me. The students were literally hanging to the walls, having banked and festooned themselves upon every conceivable article of furniture in order to hear the great leader. The crowd was immense.

"Ah," thought I, "Sun will have a hard time addressing this great over-packed hall! I wonder if his voice will reach."

Sun, after a few preliminaries, came forward.

246

There was a thunder of applause, and he stood silent for a long time, just as he always stood when I came and went at his home. He took a step forward, and the thunder of applause broke out anew in wild huzzas and terrific roars of welcome. He waited and then raised his hand. The surging crowd about was still and motionless when that hand was raised. The tick of the clock was now distinctly heard. I could hear the man next to me breathing. Sun still remained silent, with his hand raised, motionless as a statue. Then he spoke.

I hardly knew the voice. It had a new tone in it, sudden and slashing, higher pitched and with an electric emotion that held me spellbound. Charged with sincerity and truth, every word quick, rapid, accurate, acute, came like a bullet from a machine gun—*tap-tap-tap*—a clear, musical rhythm that thrilled and fascinated; now fast, now abating; now low, now high; but ever with a steady flow of language, until the voice sank suddenly with a clear, final phrasing, and he again stood silent while the echo of his voice still slashed its broad, clear argument into the minds of his hearers.

Salvos of applause broke forth from the crowd, but Sun stood there as though he were by the seashore, looking out over the waves, dreaming as

247

he watched the changing line of horizon. Then he raised his hand and the great, vociferous crowd again became a ponderous, slow-moving mass as it settled breathlessly back into close silence; again the eloquent artillery of words shot with unerring cadence, true to its mark; then again a pause and again a thunder of applause. This time Sun made his climax in the narrow range of, perhaps, half a thousand words.

The scene was as dramatic as an engaged battle-field. I stood enthralled, and even the little boy on my shoulder declared that he preferred to endure the discomfort of his cramped position rather than leave the meeting.

As the very windows rattled with applause, I thought how that same voice had carried the message of justice to the far ends of the earth—eloquent through hardships, clear-ringing amid dangers during the progress from one strange land to another—and as I followed the quick tones of his eloquence, I could hear, in the flash of my fancy, a new applause echoing from those distant parts where Sun had drawn and given the inspiration of his long struggle against the forces of evil that held the land of his birth.

"That was a good speech you made last night, Doctor," I remarked to him the next day; and

Sun, in his usual impersonal way, replied quietly:
"It was a good audience."

From the time I first heard Sun speak publicly,
he became a new man to me. I learned to know
him as never before. He was a great magician
who could charm people with his voice more easily than the Hindu fakir holds the cobra under
the spell of his rude flute. Magnetism and truth,
these were Sun's stock in trade. Sun's magnetism would do no good if he were not truthful;
but his soul and his voice, through the unerring
respect that man has for truth, made him a leader
among men.

We of the West expect our public men to be
men of a sense of humor; but they are not always
what we expect them to be. For the wit of an
Abraham Lincoln, we have the taciturnity of a
Washington, and there was only one signer of
the Declaration of Independence who cracked a
joke during the execution of the instrument.

With public men of China we find no such
popular demand for sense of humor. Confucius,
the model of all Chinese, never made a pun, never
cracked a joke, never spun a funny yarn. You
might as well have expected our Saviour to in-
ject humor into His parables as to expect a
Chinese schooled in the proprieties of the classics

249

to go about as a jokesmith. From his childhood, Sun took life seriously. He always had to be on the defensive, and for thirty years, so to speak, slept with one eye open. About the only times that he felt he was fully safe during that long generation of playing against the enemy in the dark was when he was haranguing his followers at home or abroad, in the secret chambers of their Chinese lodges. When the paraphernalia of the lodge and the emblems of its order were put aside, he knew that beyond the portal of that refuge of safety there might be the hand of an enemy waiting to do him to death.

He numbered his friends and followers by the hundreds, and eventually by the thousands and tens of thousands, but these, for the most part, were poor, while his enemies were powerful, with the means of the world's most numerous empire at their command. It is a wonder that he ever escaped from the dagger, the pistol, and the poison of his powerful enemies. He never would have escaped had he not been a man of silence. Loquacity or even over-sociability would have worked his doom. It is likewise a wonder that he was not done to death from dissensions within his own ranks. Thirty years is a long time to go about planning the upset of a mighty empire. Promises had to be made. Yes, even pledges had to be given to keep the machine of the great secret conspiracy for freedom moving. Here again Sun the Silent showed the diplomacy and genius of his leadership. He never made a promise nor gave a pledge. He let his lieutenants do that for him, and then he worked with them for earnest fulfilment.

Sun the Silent is the greatest fraternity organizer the world has ever known. He believed in the efficacy of the secret society as an instrument of warfare against the Manchus. Secret fraternities mean utter silence at discreet moments. Therefore, Sun the Eloquent, Sun the silver-tongued orator of three different languages, became Sun the Silent, when it was needful for him so to be.

Sun built up a secret fraternal organization compared with which our own great American efforts appear, indeed, small. Ramifying eventually into all parts of the globe, the nerve network of this tremendous power centered in his own leadership and moved with him as he wandered about the world during those long thirty years.

It is no wonder, then, that Sun, by the very necessity of self-preservation, has become a man of silence. He has become so used to silence that he actually enjoys it, and before I had worked with him long I also found relief in remaining still and thinking of what had been said and what remained to be said. Sometimes we would sit together for two or three moments, each with his mind busy, glancing toward each other now and then, but always silent, until each mind was prepared for the use of the words which would serve it as a vehicle for the thought assembled during silence.

But in spite of his taciturnity and reticence, Sun has, for a Chinese, a very well-developed sense of humor. He never cracks a joke, but he enjoys one and particularly the joke expressed by a whole situation. To illustrate:

The Reformer came down to my house to dinner one night, and I brought in one of my little sons, who idolized Dr. Sun. This little son was attending the Shanghai Municipal School at that time, which, being patronized mostly by the British, had as a natural part of its instruction the singing of British patriotic songs. When the lad was asked to recite or sing, I was rather discomfited by having him break forth most lustily into a rousing English song in which the chorus gave a challenge to the whole world and declared that "England rules the waves." So earnest was the child's delivery of the song and so increasingly poignant my own discomfiture that even before the song was ended Sun broke out into hearty laughter, in which we all joined, while the boy, absorbed in his song, continued his lyrical praise to England as the ruler of the world. The idea of an American boy singing songs in praise of England rather than of his own country fitted Sun's sense of humor as it eventually did mine— much to the wonderment of the lad, who had expected applause rather than laughter.

Sun the Silent has lived much of his life alone, in spite of his intense political activity; but, far from having any of that moroseness that comes from following for years a given idea, his spirit is cheerful. I have never known him to be impatient except once. He had advanced some money on a propaganda printing contract, by which the other party refused to abide. Some of Sun's followers came to me and asked my professional advice as to what to do to compel either a return of the money or a compliance with the obligations of the contract. I went to the telephone and asked Sun what his pleasure was in the matter.

"I will have nothing to do with those men," he declared in a tone which was new to me. "My patience is exhausted, and please tell my representatives to drop the whole matter."

"I can get the money back for you," I declared. (It was a substantial amount.)

"I don't want my money back," he responded. "I want neither their goods nor my money back. Let them keep the money. If I took the money back I should be having something to do with them, which is what I don't want."

So I let the fellows go scot-free from their obligation, for I knew that when Sun the Silent broke his silence it was a conclusive decision.

To know Sun well you must see him twice: once as a man of silence, sitting like a meditative Buddha, motionless in the quiet of his own reflection, and then as the orator, now swaying the multitude as a mother carries her child, and now as a general leading forces into action. When you have seen these two, so widely different, I think that you will agree that "he joins the silver of oratory to the golden eloquence of silence."

If there is any weakness in Sun Yat Sen, it is the weakness of forgiveness. With the example of the gentle Galilean before us, as men of the West, forbearance and a forgiving spirit mean strength, not weakness; but among the Chinese, with the ferocious models of the savage Manchus' conquest during two centuries, the Chinese who forgive their enemy to-day may be saving up a barrel of trouble for to-morrow. If it had not been for his forgiving attitude, Sun would perhaps be to-day the military dictator of China and would, with the power of his sway, hold the whole world under the threat of the Chinese people.

It is hard to understand 'why Sun—a man hounded about the globe, disappointed at every turn he took for thirty long years—is so soft-hearted. Any one with a half-plausible hard-luck story can have something of his sympathy and something from his pocketbook. I have known Sun to help men who were frauds, and do it merely because he felt sorry for them! His heart simply gets the best of him, and he can't help himself. He knew they were frauds, but they were unfortunate; so Sun helped them. I think that if Sun should catch, red-handed, some one trying to make an attempt upon his life, if the miscreant had a numerous family and showed any sort of disposition to be repentant, Sun would waive the incident and actually be-friend the man who had tried to destroy him.

Now, this forgiveness at first struck me as childlike. I could not understand why an iron-willed man like Sun would be so womanly and soft. His strength of will and his weakness of heart were a contrast that I could not at first reconcile. When I got to know the intimate working of his mind, this apparent weakness be-

255

came one of the strongest resources of his nature. He forgave because he was great. He forgave the boys who wrenched his queue in the Honolulu school, just as he forgave Yuan the Red for the backyard murder of Chang. It is in his nature to forgive, and long before he had ever heard of the greatest of all forgivers, Christ, he had been in the business of forgiving with a will.

I really believe that Sun Yat Sen's lifelong policy of forgiving put back in a considerable degree the constructive work that he had outlined for the Republic which he founded. If Sun had less of the forgiving quality in his soul he would probably be the undisputed President of the Chinese Republic to-day. Forgiveness is a good policy in the West with our highly evolved scheme of morality, but to the negative mind of a Chinese forgiveness, in many instances, means a lack of discrimination that spells eventual failure.

Sun the Orator; Sun the Silent; Sun the Forgiving—who shall say which is the greatest of these three? I myself can only say that forgiveness with Sun is as natural as water flowing out of a fountain. He was born forgiving, but he made himself, of his own will, an orator as well as a master, commanding the silence of his own tongue.

# XXXI

## SUN AND HWANG HSING

THIS sketch of General Hwang belongs, very properly, in this particular period of Sun's life (as far as this volume goes), not only because the period of their greatest friendship is covered by the dates of this period, but because it was one of Sun's methods to assist other strong leaders in the revolutionary movement, regardless of whether he advanced his leadership or not.

Without Hwang's military activity, it is doubtful if even Sun with his genius could have overthrown the Manchus as he did; so shall we not venture to say that if there had been no Sun there would have been no Hwang Hsing, and if there had been no Hwang Hsing the Manchus, still supported by the foreigners, would to-day be ensconced in the idle luxury of the Forbidden City, receiving homage at the Peacock Throne.

However that may be, there is, in the story of Hwang Hsing's life (or such fragments of it as we possess), something to thrill the school-boy, to stimulate the ambition of youth, to fire the imagination of the patriot, to encourage the soldier in battle advance, and to hold in long reverie the meditations of the philosopher. Yes, Hwang's life is a theme for a battle-hymn and a motif to inspire the dramatic genius of a Shakspere or to satisfy the dramatic imagination of a Wagner. For Hwang's whole life thrilled with the courage of his great soul.

Sun was the diplomat, the originator, a political Christopher Columbus who threw the line of his perspective out so far that his genius alone saw to its very end. Hwang was the restless soldier, ever eager for battle, calculating deeply from experience, but always ready to risk his life on any chance that appealed to his dramatic instinct of bravery. Sun thrilled thousands with his oratory; Hwang took these inspired thousands, and with the battle-cry of his leadership he stormed the fortress or swept on to victory over the bloody field of battle. Hwang is a natural leader; so is Sun. But the psychology of the two is different; hence, Providence brought the twain together in a common effort that will be recognized eventually as a service for all humanity. Put Hwang in the forecastle of a ship and he becomes the leader of the whole crew by his example of physical prowess and by the sheer force of his intrepidity and personal courage.

Put Sun in the forecastle of a ship, and he leads the whole crew by the simple exercise of his mental magnetism. Sun's way is the easy way of reason; Hwang's is the harder and less certain way of force. Hwang is the master-gunner stripped to the waist, confident of his marksmanship as he discerns in the roar and din of battle the weak point of his enemy. Sun is the pilot who, aloft on the open bridge, considers rather the course of his ship than the detailed action of the guns.

Hwang sees near; Sun sees far. Hwang's hand is ever on his sword, and as swift as a flash of fire comes his challenge of death. Sun never uses force if there is still a reasoned chance of parley. Hwang's great courage only finds its expression in open combat; to him a battle is like a feast, and the red deluge of carnage comes like rich wine to stimulate his supreme courage further. Most leaders of Hwang's type find defeat rather than victory, but this calculating genius gives battle against the most desperate odds, and, at that, never suffers any worse defeat than a draw; for he measures the length of his sword at every exchange of blows.

It was in Japan in 1906 that these two saw the speck of hope in China's clouded political sky that eventually was to grow from the size of a man's hand to the full arch of clear day; and it was only five years later, on December 14, 1911, that Hwang Hsing was appointed by the provisional parliament of the Chinese Republic to act as President until the arrival of Sun Yat Sen, to whom he delivered over the chief magistracy.

In 1906 Hwang had fled from China to Japan with a price on his head. So had Sun. Sun believed that he was now in a position to extend his organization work right up to the very walls of the imperial yamens. So did Hwang. Hence, they joined hands as never before, and each knew now that success would attend his efforts. They beheld, at length, their imperial opponent like a weary pugilist holding on to the ropes while waiting for the knock-out blow. It would still take years, but they would be years of hope and not years of despair like those before the Boxer uprising. The old Manchu ring champion, with his purple girdle befouled, with ten generations of blood, would before long have to take the count. He might still have enough force to down his opponent for a brief moment, but age and the infirmities of dissipations were at length counting upon him, and the champions of the new republic were now ready to let loose a double-barreled pair of uppercuts that would knock the old eunuch of the ring limp and lifeless; and knock him out they did, in that finally successful revolution commenced at Wuchang, in the Province of Hupeh, on October 10, 1911.

Hwang was born in 1875. Sun was nearly ten years older. It was not on account of this seniority, however, that Hwang looked up to Sun. Sun was a product of both the East and the West. Hwang Hsing was solely a product of the East, never having had any western education. His academic education was obtained in the state college of the two Hu provinces, from which he graduated with high honors, and then, as a postgraduate course, entered the Japanese Tokyo University, from which he graduated, likewise with distinction. May we not find interest in a conjecture as to what Hwang Hsing would have been had he had the Occidental education that Sun possesses? Hwang, the Hunanese, recognized the leadership of Sun, the Cantonese, because Hwang a leader himself, knew that only through Sun could the order of better things be accomplished. And Sun, in his turn, knew that it was upon Hwang Hsing's support that he would have to rely for the continuance of his program during the long periods of his banishment. For, as the years rolled along, Sun's banishment came to be more and more under the surveillance not only of the Manchus but of certain Christian nations as well. In 1904 the Im-

261

perial Throne, finding that it was making little headway against Sun's revolution, bethought itself to take the wind out of his sails by issuing a proclamation of amnesty to all revolutionists, as an act of grace shown by the empress dowager on the occasion of her seventieth birthday; she, however, declared that there were three revolutionists who should never be forgiven: Sun Yat Sen, Kung Hu Wei, and Liang Chi Chao. With this ban against Sun, he counted more and more upon Hwang.

So Sun and Hwang, while they were refugees in Japan, during the two years preceding the time covered by the chapter entitled "No. 121 Under the Hillside," formed the Patriots' Association. When this organization was fully formed, the Dare-to-Dies came out of their swaddling-clothes and donned the heavy steel armor of battle for a fight to the bitterest end. Just as Sun was a natural leader of the theory of the whole revolution, so Hwang was the natural leader of the courageous practices of the Dare-to-Dies; for the Dare-to-Die movement, with its myriads of dangers, was all in the day's work to Hwang.[1] Hwang went about his labor with the

[1] The above does not mean that Sun was merely the intellectual leader of the Manchu overthrow. Sun became a practical Dare-to-Die in the attack which we have mentioned as of the medley date "Ninth Moon, 1895," and risked his life with astonishing

cheerful courage of the man who reflects, "We must die, so let us die bravely." At that Hwang prepared his men to sell their lives only at the dearest price.

It was fortunate that Hwang and Sun were in Japan when the Dare-to-Die movement finally took on something of the momentum which at length was to develop into such a terrific force; they could train the Dare-to-Dies better in Japan than in China. Japan, just emerging from the feudal era, was a land of swordsmen, where excellent instruction could be had on every hand. The Japanese are a very brave people; and Japan, as the land of *bushido,* offered an inspiration to this self-sacrificing, patriotic movement. The natural weapon of the Dare-to-Dies was the short, sharp sword, for it was always loaded, readily concealed and easy to replace.

About middle stature, General Hwang possessed the long arms of the natural heavy swordsman and the shifty, quick legs of the foil-fencer.

frequency in subsequent Dare-to-Die movements of hand-to-hand conflict, of which the narration is not permitted in the brevity of this volume. The above does mean, however, that as Sun's revolutionary movement gained momentum and while he was busy gathering together the "sinews of war," he inspirited brave leaders to the combative action of the Dare-to-Die. Chief among these was General Hwang Hsing. Space does not permit paying homage to other courageous Chinese revolutionary heroes, but this sketch of General Hwang Hsing is essential to give the reader an idea of the nobility and bravery of the courageous captains, who made possible Sun's program of Chinese liberation.

He was built "down on the ground," with a great, square head, bulging deep chest, powerful yet supple shoulders; and in Japan he would pass easily as a professional wrestler because of his bulk and natural agility of limb and body.

Chinese generally do not look like soldiers, but Hwang did, in spite of the fact that he always insisted on wearing his foreign uniforms so loose and baggy that, without looking at the head above them, one would have laughed at their grotesqueness. When he put on afternoon attire—the dinner-coat or full dress—he had clothes that fitted him in the close, restricted foreign fashion; but putting on a uniform, to Hwang, meant getting ready for a fight, and when Hwang fought, you may be sure that he wanted nothing that would retard the suppleness of his action. Hwang had faced death too often to want to give the other fellow the single hairbreadth of an unnecessary advantage. Not that Hwang did not give his adversary a full and fair chance, but Hwang figured, in his Dare-to-Die fashion, that a fight meant that one side had to die; and Hwang always made up his mind before he gave the command to advance that the dying should have to be done by the enemy. It was a cruel, hard philosophy, but it has had the indorsement of twenty centuries of Christian civilization, so that we cannot blame this great Chinese general for applying it with the extreme vigor—yes, ruthlessness—that turned the Manchu hordes into a red shambles of despair. Hwang, outnumbered, never hesitated to take a chance to out-manœuver the enemy, and he is not to be censured if, in the fury of battle, he tapped a little harder than necessary on the head of his enemy in order to make the victory doubly certain. Hwang developed his military prowess on the theory that the enemy was always stronger than he, and that therefore he should have to act more quickly and take greater chances than his adversary, which clearly accounts for the terrific mortality of the brave men who followed him.

It was undoubtedly these soldierly qualities of Hwang and the inspiration of confidence in them that brought the Chinese capitalist guilds of the provinces of Hunan and Hupeh to revolutionary support for the great blow that finally was to be struck successfully in October, 1911.

If Hwang led his men to death, however, he was always dared to die. If they took one chance, Hwang took two. They believed in Hwang, and Hwang believed in his Dare-to-Dies; in that superlatively beautiful cast of courage that Sun's revolutions developed, it was a case of "Here's a cup for the dead already, and hurrah for the next man to die!"

For years Sun had believed that if he could capture the vice-imperial yamen at Canton he could use its revenue to build up an attack against the Imperialists all over China; it was to him the hammer with which to pound out his foes on every anvil of their refuge. So for years Sun had planned attack after attack against this rich and well-fortified yamen, at times, personally directing the assault himself. Every time he had failed. Now Sun in banishment at last saw the great chance; Hwang Hsing would carry through to success the plan that had so many times failed.

So on April 27, 1911, Hwang was at last ready. The Dare-to-Dies were armed, equipped, and disciplined as never before. It was to have been a sudden and quick attack. Alas! through that treachery so frequent in China, the Imperialist commander in Canton learned of the movement and immediately put himself in a position of full defense. Prudence now demanded the retreat of the Dare-to-Dies, for the Manchu troops had been so reinforced that it appeared folly even to approach them. Hwang the Intrepid, however, scoffed at the proposal to retire. If the enemy was so very much stronger than he, then he would

make up in swiftness of action what he lacked in
number; if the enemy were so much better armed
than he, then he must possess himself of the
enemy's arms. All things were possible to brave
men; and, besides, he had been promised reinforcements. He would take the yamen, and then
the reinforcements would come to help him hold
it. At all events, even if the reinforcements did
not arrive, then Hwang would fight his way out
—as he would fight his way in—and show the
enemy, at all events, that they had to deal with
men of valor and that he was afraid neither of
mere numbers nor of superiority of weapons.
When a man was a Dare-to-Die he could not be
a coward, and Sun and Hwang had always declared in the Association of Patriots that they had
no room for poltroons in their following. Moreover, it was better to die gloriously in an assault
on the yamen than to violate the oaths which they
had so solemnly taken.

So Hwang, in full face of an apparently certain death, gave the command to advance, and
with Hwang at their very head, the brave band
stormed the viceroy's yamen and, over a wall of
dead and dying, possessed themselves of the point
of vantage.

Every hour of that whole long day that Hwang
held the yamen was an epic of bravery told in

dramatic chapters of a thrilling tragedy of courage. Time after time the Manchus attacked, until the walls of the yamen groaned with the shock of the onslaught; each time a screaming, cursing, bloody mass of Imperialists retreated before the Dare-to-Die flash of the sword and crash of the carbine, while every hour the windrows of dead grew higher. The yamen had now become a blood-flowing slaughter-pen within, and a red shambles of horror without. But there stood Hwang Hsing, calm, grim-visaged, watching the crash of each shell and counting his dead as they fell, in the counter-attack which he ordered at every fresh onslaught. He was crimson with the blood of his enemies, of his fallen comrades, and of his own wounds. A part of one hand was chopped away. He directed the application of the tourniquet and helped stanch the flow of his blood with the *sang-froid* of a boy sopping his bread in jam; then, taking his sword in the other hand, he again led the affray.

It was supreme, it was wonderful to those who love the dramatic, but to matter-of-fact Hwang it was just a mere incident in the life of a Dare-to-Die. He realized, in spite of his dizziness from loss of blood, that things were going badly with his band; still he hung on and fought as he waited.

"The reinforcements—will they come?"

The crash of shrapnel, the crack of rifles, the red spit of the carbine, walls that trembled and floors that creaked under the ever-increasing weight of the dead; groans, shrieks, screams and curses. . . . and there, in the midst of the crimson bedlam of carnage stands Hwang Hsing, calmly pausing for a moment in the lull of the battle, now . . . to count his living. It was the Alamo all over again, but on a larger and more horrible scale.

"Men, the night advances, and under its cover we shall cut our way out; the reinforcements have failed us."

There was no bitterness in the tone; I do not think that it ever occurred to Hwang, in his courageous self-possession, that he could not cut his way out with the Dare-to-Dies still surviving, just as he had slashed his way in.

"Forward!"

With one supreme effort the Dare-to-Dies throw themselves against the Manchu wall of soldiery, who, bewildered at the suddenness of the attack, for a moment double back on their comrades, thus giving Hwang's men a chance to get the desired opening. Carbines, rifles, and pistols are now thrown aside; even the bayonet becomes cumbersome in those densely packed ranks of friend and foe, while the trenching-knife and pick gleam in the dim light of the torches and fall in sickening cuts and thuds upon that cursing, groaning, struggling human herd.

And now there is a movement like the slow beginning of a whirlpool in the midst of that screaming, bloody, crowd. It is the effort of the living to get away from the center of a maelstrom quickly forming in the depth of the mass of struggling men, now helpless because of the great pressure that ever pushes it outward; and in the very center we behold Hwang in the flare of the torches, circling about like a gunner in the cockpit, behind a parapet of dead; and in the clearing of this space, we see the sword dealt by his unwounded hand, rising and falling, feinting and countering, all the time clearing and widening that precious space that will eventually mean liberty in the outer darkness just beyond.

"Comrades, follow me! This is the way through."

The Dare-to-Dies who still survive turn to follow the square, bull-like figure, goring its way forward at the point of the flashing sword; but, alas! another movement of the dense mass of soldiery, and Hwang, still fighting desperately, is carried in one direction and the survivors of his band in another: It is no longer a battle; it is a crimson flood. Alas! although Hwang the Invincible fights his way out, the brave survivors are surrounded, some immediately dispatched, and something under a hundred made prisoners.

Out in the safety of the night, Hwang, like a wounded mother tiger, haunts the darkness in a hope that reinforcements will come so that he may rescue his captured comrades. His own wounds have made him weak, but there is no rest or sleep for him. One of the Dare-to-Dies who has escaped with him gives his wounds another first-aid dressing, tourniqueting the bleeding stumps of his fingers and bandaging the bleeding wounds on his head. Then Hwang, in the cool of the evening, turns his face to the river breeze to assuage his fever and waits. Some men would have complained, others ranted, still others would have brooded. Hwang just sat and waited.

The din of the bloody day's work still continued in the echoes of the night as the dead were carted off, and the flickering of torches on the slopes beyond the walls showed the searching-parties looking for Hwang and his handful of survivors. Hwang was weak, and his fever ran high; otherwise, I think that he would have followed those searching-parties, one by one, and cut them, single-handed, to pieces. Alas! even Hwang the Intrepid realized, as his weakness grew with his loss of blood, that there was to be no rescue for the few survivors of his band. The next morning these brave men—Dare-to-Dies to the last—to the number of threescore and ten, were beheaded cruelly upon the execution-grounds of Canton.

Such is one of the tales of the bravery of Hwang, one of the greatest hand-to-hand fighters of all time, whose genius as a leader of large forces was inspired by his own personal courage. I now reflect with sorrow that so little can be found to tell the whole story of his great courageous life.

I say with sorrow, for I once had the opportunity to perform a service to posterity by gathering up the first-hand story of Hwang's campaigns; but, alas, Death, by reason of my own procrastination, cheated me of this great chance! I met him in Chicago in 1914, after he had been driven out of China by Yuan the Red. He had come to America from Japan. Our meeting was joyful, for I had known Hwang for years in the spirit, and Hwang had long known something good of me. Now there he stood by my side in the flesh, in appearance just as I had always fancied him through those years.

He had one of those suites of the great hotel that looks out over Lake Michigan. After the first glad salutations, we stepped over by some

Weary days are spent in traveling even a hundred miles.

The ubiquitous umbrella accompanies all Chinese travelers, for they never know when and where shall come the end of the tedious journey. From the very beginning Sun urged upon his followers the need of railroads.

Two representative types of Chinese Nationalists (Sun's followers). It was among such coura-geous men as these that the author labored (Page 205).

common impulse and stood looking at each other; then Hwang waved his sword-chopped hand out toward the lake:

"It is peaceful here."

I, too, looked out over the lake. Verily, it was peaceful. The sound of the auto-horn instead of the call of the bugle; the low mingled tone of the street traffic instead of the heavy rumble of the artillery-train; and then, beyond, on the lake, itself, no gunboats, no frowning fortresses. Yes, it was peace.

"It is grand to be in your land of peace." (At that time we were at peace with the whole world, while the continent of Europe was being drenched with blood.)

So that day we talked more of peace than of war; delightful questionings and answers. Alas! if I had only known the precious time that I was wasting!

"After I get out this new book, General, I shall write the story of your campaigns. When we go back to China, I want to go to some Buddhist convent, one of those mountain philosophy places —Taichan, or, perhaps, the sanctuary of Pou Tou Island—and there, in the liberty of isolation, I shall write a good and true story of your life. We shall spend a week or so together, and then you shall leave me alone with your maps and plans

273

and data, and come back in six months and tell me if the book be true and good.''

Ah, how vain are the confident predictions of man!

''I am going to Media to-night. Perhaps you may visit us there.'' Up to that time I had never heard of Media, Pennsylvania, but since General Hwang made that his place of refuge in America, it has always been to me a place of great respect.

''General,'' I responded, ''there is no background for the biography of a life such as yours here in America. I want to make a good book. I can't write here in America; there are too many interruptions. This book should be written in some hermit place in China.''

There was a long pause. Foolishly I had let my enjoyment in meeting Hwang dull the quicker activities of my mind; I did not think even to ask Hwang if the invitation really meant that I should have an opportunity for that constant association that meant making a book of a man's life. That long pause was one of the greatest lost opportunities of my life. It was I who broke it; I said foolishly and with no reflection whatsoever:

''General, when you get to Media, please write me something that I can use as a foundation; something that will start the work here, and

274

make the anticipation of its accomplishment more real, when we are together in China.''

It was a fatuous remark, a mere platitude. Why could not I have used the deeper channels of my brain in that momentous moment? As I reflect now, my sense was all sheer nonsense in failing to have a clearer understanding of Hwang's program in exile.

''I shall send you something. If you publish it, it will do our cause great good,'' said Hwang in a matter-of-fact way; and I, still in an indolence of mental activity, simply responded:

''I shall greatly appreciate this friendly service, General.''

So then we entered into the social visit. My wife was with me, and the cordial relations established between her and the general's beautiful daughter soon developed that happy feeling of social confidence that brought Hwang and me even closer together.

Then, with heartfelt *au revoirs,* we separated. Yes, it would only be a short time before we met again.

My wife and I went out into the marble hallway and stood waiting for the lift.

''Wait a moment, please,'' I said to my wife. ''There is something that I forgot to ask the general.''

I went back to the door we had just left. It was ajar, and through the angle of the opening I saw Hwang, with his beautiful daughter poising herself lightly upon the arm of the great fauteuil in which Hwang was seated. She was holding his hand in hers, while they talked together in low, serious tones.

I tapped at the door, and from the depths of the cushions Hwang came to his feet in a slow, graceful, ceremonious way.

"Sorry, General, but I just came back to say—" And then the apparent foolishness of the return came upon me, and I could only add as I grasped the unmutilated hand, "General, I just wanted to say 'au revoir' again."

Long we looked at each other; then we parted, and this time (alas, had I only had some definite premonition!) we parted forever.

Some little time after this, I received a bulky package from Hwang. I think my fingers must have trembled as I opened it. Therein lay (as I thought) what was to serve as the foundation of the life-story of one of the bravest of generals. I opened the package carefully, like the pilgrim opening a sacred book.

It was a long, typewritten document gotten up in that formal way that means much to the Chinese, but which to us of the West, with our love of detail, means little, if anything; and in this document Hwang Hsing made no mention of himself. It was an appeal to the American public to lend its support to Chinese democracy against the usurpation of Yuan. I was grievously disappointed but used it in a book I was then writing for the Chinese Nationalists.

That this disappointment did not stir me up to make a sustained and patient effort to get as much as possible of a detailed story of General Hwang's life, will always be a great regret to me. I procrastinated under the excuse of many other things to do, with the result that when I again got back to my original purpose the startling news came that General Hwang Hsing, the great combatant of China's successful revolution, was dead.

When I returned to China I went to present my condolences to his widow and to some of the other relatives of the family. In the hearty Chinese fashion, Mrs. Hwang Hsing gave an elaborate dinner to me and the family. She concurred heartily in my plan to get up something of a sketch biography of her husband; but Chinese proprieties in regard to the family are peculiar. Moreover, Mrs. Hwang Hsing was busy in a multitude of charitable and patriotic undertakings, and I did not dare to presume further upon her good-heartedness; so, with a final attempt to obtain definite information of the details of Hwang Hsing's campaigns, I was (with the hope that sometime I should have a providential fund of information) compelled to abandon the plan. The general's widow finally sold her beautiful house in Shanghai and went back to her home in the provinces to live. It has been a number of years since I had the honor of hearing from her. She is, indeed, a beautiful character and fortunate in having a talented and numerous family to console her in the loss of her illustrious husband.

General Hwang Hsing died in the prime of life. What his enemies on the field of battle could not do, disappointment and wrecked patriotic hopes accomplished. His exile to Japan and America wore heavily upon him. Inaction, to him, was poisoned air. The duty he knew was that of courageous advance. Take this away from him and he was like the King Lion of the wide desert, pacing the narrow confines of a cage and ever gazing far away in the vain hope of again seeing the great range of his lost activity. He would have rejoiced a Washington and inspired a Napoleon with his supreme courage.

The vision of Hwang frequently rises before me, and I see him, as I saw him in that upholstered chair. Grim of visage, dogged, determined, with a deep gaze that ever called defiance to the enemies of China, this man of courage, who had proved his mastery in a hundred bloody encounters, held in his sword-chopped hand the hand of his daughter and smiled back at her smile like a happy child.

Even in the comfort and love of his family circle, Hwang Hsing brooded over the wrongs of his country. Upholstered chairs were not for him when tyrants ruled China, but rather the hard, stony couch of a soldier on the march, ready to strike camp by the gleam of the stars in order the quicker to attack the enemy.

I think that all of us who have had the privilege of knowing a great mind have a feeling of loneliness when we learn of its light going out. As the years roll along I seem to have a better understanding of Hwang from the deep impression that his strong personality left upon me. Again and again I reproach myself: "Had it not been for my procrastination I would have cheated Death of the mystery of the romantic details that have now gone with Hwang to his tomb."

I went out to the home of the dead general's family for the memorial exercises of the second anniversary of his death. In the beautiful, wide sweep of the center hallway, they had built up an altar of the most fragrant flowers, in the midst of which, Chinese fashion, was a large framed picture of Hwang Hsing. Breathing in the deep perfume of the flowered midst, in the silence of the moment, I gazed long at the picture, although it was, indeed, familiar to me, since Hwang himself had given me one of the originals when the likeness was first taken.

I approached nearer, coming deeper into the thick fragrance of the flowers, and as I stood and reflected, to me the spot, for the time being, became dedicated to the higher purposes of that great courage for which Hwang's whole life was a supreme ideal.

As I lingered, the little baby boy of the great general toddled over to me and looked wonderingly. I took the child by the hand; and, governed by some instinct, common alike to the babe, to the mature, and to the aged, the little one stood patiently beside me while I still remained at that place, sanctified to the spirit of courage as symbolized in the memory of Hwang Hsing.

Hwang Hsing, the leader of the Dare-to-Dies, was dead. Hwang Hsing, who carried on the work of blood and who took the brunt of battle because he believed in Chinese liberty; Hwang the Indomitable; Hwang the Courageous; Hwang the Upright Patriot; Hwang, who threw his life a hundred times in the balance because he, with Sun, saw visions of better things for the land he loved—this man whose courage shone like a light had gone where Peace reigned. The sword-chopped hand I had touched with the light pressure of that deep friendship of the inner being, the low suppressed voice, the deep gleam of eyes that shone as lava ready to break into a stream of fire, the powerful block-like figure of the quick swordsman—all this came back to me, as the wondering child stood by my side.

There came upon me a rhapsody of grief. I did not prostrate myself, as had some of those who had gone before me, but I smiled as I walked from the perfumed midst of that flowered altar, raised to the dead, while the little child wondered at the emotion I showed.

Verily, when a great soul goes out, the world is lonely, but glad in the remembrance of what that soul has done.

# XXXII

A STRANGE fact of Sun's development into the eventual human force which would break down the tyranny of the Manchus is that he began his work as a child from the genius of his own mind and leadership, with nothing else to help him.

If we study the lives of other great political reformers, we shall find that they have always had some family, or clan, or tribal motive at the base of their hatred of the oppressor, but we have seen how Sun's family stood against him in his efforts at reform. I think that, along this line, the following episode will prove perhaps as interesting to the reader as it did to me.

There had been a collateral uncle in the Sun family to whom Sun's mother had been much endeared. He was a prominent member of the family circle, and through his ambitious persistence he got his family to support him in seeking a political office. It took a long time to get the

282

job, but finally came the glad tidings that he had
been appointed as a small official in the under-
offices of the Ningpo yamen. Ah, what a wonderful day for the Sun family. Long and glad was
the merry feasting in the family circle. At last
a member of the Sun family was to enter the
mysterious realm of the service of the Son of
Heaven and at Ningpo, the great city of a hundred
wonders. Ah, at last one member was on the
direct highway to opulence and honor! He sailed
off with a smiling face and a light heart amid the
glad congratulations of the numerous members of
the Sun family, upon whom he would, as they
hoped, shower the honors of officialdom. Yes, the
Sun family was getting on in the world of the
mandarinate.

Alas! holding office under the mandarinate was
not the bed of roses of which he had dreamed.
This simple enthusiast of the Blue Valley stood
no chance against the machinations of the harpies
of the Ningpo yamen, and so, after severe af-
flictions and protracted tribulations, he was
driven out in disgrace.

Far from home, stranded, and in great straits,
it was only with difficulty that he finally returned
to Blue Valley broken and disconsolate. Glad,
indeed, was he to get back again, as self-effacing
as the Prodigal Son as he entered upon the hard

labor of the field. The villagers wagged their heads wisely and attributed his misfortune to the "bad joss" of political office.

The return of the broken man made a strong impression upon the mind of the mother of the Reformer, and whenever she would grow uneasy over the Reform discussions of her beloved son she would lament:

"Wen, remember that it is unlucky for any of the Sun family to hold office. Bear ever in mind the misfortune that befell your uncle in Ningpo. All politics is naught. Politics means failure."

When Sun quoted his mother's words to me, his voice sounded low and subdued. It was such a good story that I smiled. But I stopped smiling when I saw the seriousness of Sun's face. To me it had been an amusing tale. To him it had been a tragedy in the family circle, from which had grown a text of admonishment that, from his memory, had been preached to him all his life:

"Remember your uncle in Ningpo. All politics is naught. Politics means failure."

Yes, indeed, familiar was that text to him.

It was at the close of a long hot day that Sun casually, yet earnestly, told me this tale, when we had come out into the cool of the balcony to enjoy the breeze of the evening and to partake of refreshment. After Sun had ended the episode

284

with the words slowly and earnestly pronounced, "My dear old mother warned me repeatedly that all politics was naught," he remained for a long time silent. As we sat in the twilight and looked out over the flower-garden, I saw a new, deep look gather over his solemn face. And then, in my turn, I fell into a reverie, as the two of us sat there in the gathering night.

In my reverie I saw Sun standing in the darkness of Hong Kong's harbor on that fatal night in 1894, when he superintended the shipment of those first arms and instruments of death which he had obtained at the peril of his own life and through funds procured solely by his own eloquence. All is propitious. All goes well. Ah, the time has come to strike for freedom! Yonder, on the Canton side, wait the strong arms and the clear brains that would take these instruments of death and hurl destruction into the midst of the Manchu soldiery. Over the dark channel follows Sun. Yes, in a little while the fatal hour will come, and the brave supporters on the other side will stand with him in the glorious moment of victory for China's freedom, now so soon to arrive. After years and years of waiting, at last the blow shall be struck.

Alas! just as success is about to crown his efforts, and just as the waiting arms of his followers are about to seize these instruments of death, through the treachery of an unknown foe, the arms are discovered by the Imperialists, and the expedition ends in failure. And on the following day, when the dreadful news came that Sun's friends, Chur Se, Shun Kewi Chen, and Lu Hao Ting, had been tortured to death, did he not hear the voice of his mother saying: "Beware, Wen, beware! Politics means failure. Remember your uncle of Ningpo. Beware."

Yes, politics meant failure. All politics was naught. Beware! Beware!

Then, in my reverie in the twilight, I again saw Sun as he escaped in the darkness of Hong Kong's harbor after another thwarted effort, and fled, with a price on his head, to Japan, and then on over to Hawaii and again on to America and Europe, a hunted man and a failure. Yes, alas! politics means failure in the Sun family.

Again I saw him in the secret chambers of those Chinese sons of liberty where his revolutionary organization still goes forward, and this time with a new momentum. Among the laundrymen and the merchants, among the Chinese farmers, among the domestics, I saw him there in America developing those humble men into a new support with which again to strike for freedom. And still on he goes to Mexico and Canada. I saw him on the banks of the Thames and on the arched bridges of the Seine, scheming and devising ways to avoid those failures that have heretofore met him on every hand. Then into Russia and dipping down to the equator, with the sweep of an eagle, on to the lands of spice and cinnamon, working up, as he goes, enthusiasm for Chinese liberty on every side and accumulating a treasure with which again to purchase the instruments of death. Finally he returns to England. Ah, again disaster! There, in the darkness of the Manchu Legation in London, he awaits with calmness the death-grip of the cord of silk. Yes, after all, his mother was right. Politics means misfortune. Politics means failure. Beware!

But he escapes the silken cord of the executioners! Again he swings around the globe. Again he obtains with the silver of his voice the gold necessary to bring liberty to four hundred million people. His followers have now grown into tens of thousands. They are scattered to the four points of the compass. Most of them are of small means, and few have the skill in arms to help him on to victory. Again, he waits, and in his waiting there is failure.

"Beware of politics! All politics is naught!

Why didst thou not obey the injunction of her
who gave you being?''

And now comes the rebellion of the Righteous
Fist, a rebellion born in ignorance and fostered by
the wickedness and serpent-cunning of the dowager empress. Ah, this is the time! This is the
chance! Here is a great opportunity in this
political confusion to strike an iron blow for
Chinese liberty. But again failure, and this time
of a more serious sort.

Sun's enemies, through their influence with the
powers, have published a ban against him. No
land bordering on his beloved China is now open
to him. The foreign powers governing the seas
and shores about China declare that Sun, the
dangerous revolutionist, can no longer approach
any of their possessions.

Yes, this indeed means failure. His mother
was right: politics is naught. Why did he not
beware?

Then I saw him in the fatal year of 1910, there
in the South Sea Islands, where, with the rem-
nant of his broken and discouraged army, he
finds eventually his refuge, harassed by the
foreign powers, hunted like a miscreant by the
Manchus, and now regarded, even by his own followers, as a man broken by failure.

It is the Valley Forge of the Chinese struggle

The Shanghai Bund of 1914, showing German Club with spire.

Farther up at the French Concession on the Whangpo. It was
several miles below this that the Gunboat Drama of the
Whangpo was enacted (Page 328).

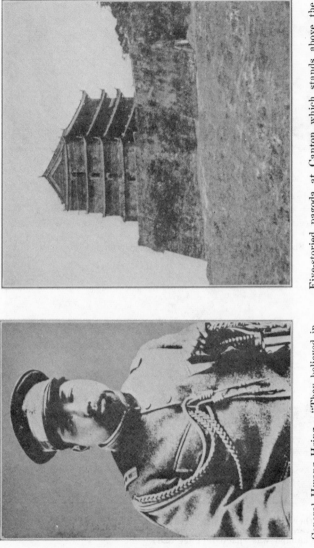

General Hwang Hsing. "They believed in Hwang, and Hwang believed in his Dare-to-Dies". (Page 265).

Five-storied pagoda at Canton which stands above the yamen where General Hwang fought April 27, 1911 (Page 266).

for independence. On the tropical shores, instead of the print of the bloody footstep in the snow, there is shadowed upon the blistering sands the zigzag foot-tracks of starving men who look grimly at their leader with eyes glazing with death and demand bread—demand bread, those proud and confident soldiers, sure of the success of their leader, who, but a few weeks before, demanded the golden prize of liberty—now in a starved and beggarly condition only ask for bread, and even this he cannot give them.

Yes, politics means naught. Why didst thou not heed the warning of her who loved thee best?

Then, in my reverie, I saw him as he stood in the midst of those sick and dying men, some of whom bore the unhealed wounds of battles, battles that ever resulted in defeat. Ah! Now again he hears the text:

"Beware, Wen! Politics means failure"; and in my reverie I see him looking down the line of those dying and starving patriots and hear him crying out:

"Yes, mother was right! I am the cause of all this suffering and misery. It is I who have broken these brave men upon the torture-wheel of my own failure. Nine times have I struck, and nine times have my blows failed. Nine times have we gone forward, only to leave a bloody toll of dead comrades upon the battle-field of our misfortune. Yes, mother was right. Politics means failure.''

With heavier prices put upon his head in his native land, and with the penalties of the law declared in foreign acts of banishment, a period of inactivity assails him. Failure has apparently, at length, conquered; failure has stripped him of his occupation. "Ah! now wilt thou not heed the admonition of thy mother?''

Yes, it is failure, but it is not despair. With a few faithful followers he seeks refuge across thousands of miles of rolling sea and continent. It is hard now for him to keep in touch with his beloved China, and with that new army of followers who are willing to lay down their lives for the cause of Chinese liberty. Out of the bitterness of his repeated failures come added determination and courage; now his following grows into the scores of thousands, but they are far away, and the messages of good cheer take long to carry. Even this new success spells failure, for the support cannot come to the Leader, and the Leader cannot go to his support. Yes, Wen, now in your utter banishment do you not realize that "politics means failure"?

Still his crusade for liberty goes on. Now, those who indorse his activity are numbered by the hundreds of thousands. This, verily, is the twelfth hour of his whole life. The banishment continues with renewed difficulties. It is declared by great Imperial China and her allies that he is to be taken either dead or alive. Even in the Christian press of the world, his enemies hurl vituperation against him. Now every gateway to his beloved China is closed to him—that China whose fields and mountain-sides have been drenched with the blood of his failure. Yes, eleven times failure, and, ah! the flash of the Manchu's pitiless sword, the precious blood that has been shed! Oh, the groans from the Tartar torture-rack, and the gush of life from the decapitated trunk! Oh, the misery of those noisome prisons where the Sons of Liberty in the same breath pray for death and the freedom of China!

"Yes, perhaps, after all, mother was right. I was doomed to failure. Poor old mother, in her love for me, in the simple tale of uncle's failure, tried to guide me. I am responsible for all this misfortune and suffering. I am responsible to all these broken men, living and dead. All this torture is mine. Mine is the guilt. I have urged these brave men on to misery and death. This is the twelfth hour."

But again his indomitable courage urges him

on. His message flashes out from under the depth of the Pacific:

"Forward! Make no delay! Capture Wuchang! This is the hour."

Yes, this is the twelfth, the final hour. Ah! will they, can they strike at last that iron blow for Chinese freedom?

Hwang Hsing the Courageous, Hwang Hsing the Intrepid takes the order. Hwang, with his Dare-to-Dies, strikes with the desperation of that final hour; and China, at last, is free!

The hour of victory which for thirty years he has awaited, finally comes. He smiles as he now hears in the recesses of his memory the chidings of his dear old mother as she warned him against the snares of political life.

Ah, dear, sweet mother! You, mother with the bound feet, but the full and untrammeled heart that not even the backward customs of two thousand years could restrain in your love! You sought the safety of your son in your way, in the footsteps of the twentieth century of ancient models. To-day your son, the leader of millions, honors you with the honors of the great, because he sought the safety of the Chinese people that you love. The uncle of Ningpo failed because his enemies were those whom your son has thrown down. If you, dear old mother, could stand forth from your carefully kept grave of to-day, where every year the prostrations of love are made, I am sure that you would say:

"Wen, we shall no longer be unlucky in politics. Through your courage the influences that overcame your uncle in Ningpo are no more."

# SEVENTH PERIOD

From January 1, 1912, to the fall of Nanking
in the Second Revolution, October 27, 1913.

PRESIDENTIAL AND POST-PRESIDENTIAL

## XXXIII

### FIRST PRESIDENT OF THE CHINESE REPUBLIC

IT WAS on Christmas eve, 1911, that Sun landed at Shanghai after thousands of miles and weary years of wandering. Again he returned to the land of his birth, but not as a disguised exile with a price upon his head. No longer did he fear the challenge of the foreign police nor the treachery of the Manchu soldiers. He returned to China amid the acclaim of the whole people, to the China that he had transformed from an empire of blood and of misery into a republic, before whose new-raised portals stood the Angel of Hope.

Although Sun and I rarely discussed religion during the many days we were together, I believe Sun in his heart is a Christian, but his is the sort of Christianity that makes all good men brothers, whether they have heard of the message of the great Nazarene or unconsciously follow it in their search for better things. He is a Christian of the whole brotherhood of man.

I believe that on that Christmas eve, as he

heard the chimes of the English cathedral at Shanghai, he thanked the True God of all men for the final deliverance of the most numerous race of the whole globe from the murderous tyranny of the Manchu. I do not think that Sun took any credit to himself; I think that he thought only of his God who had made these things possible. Sun's prayers of thirty years now became a Christian carol of praise.

Two hundred and ten miles above Shanghai, on the Asiatic Father of Waters, lies the famous and classic capital of Nanking. It was the center of administration and the residence of the six dynasties between the fourth and sixth centuries, and then, centuries later, it became the capital of the Mings. It is a great city in a fertile land, whose productive valleys and grass-grown mountains speak of the traditions of five thousand years. It was here that the forerunner of the deliverance of the Chinese, the untutored but courageous chief of the Taiping rebels, held forth for half a generation under his banner of the Great Peace, only at length to die by poison from his own hand in the red shambles of his fallen comrades. Since, at the time of his tragic end, America was in a death-struggle over the question of slavery of the blacks, I do not think that we should be harsh in judging the "long-haired rebel'' in his attempt to free his fellows from the slavery of Manchu rule.

I think that every one of those 210 miles was a Via Dolorosa to Sun. He knew the pains and the penalties, the disappointments and the sufferings that would come with the holding of the office of first President of the republic. The republic was established, but for how long? If he could only keep it together until there should be something of recognition in the councils of the world, something to show the Chinese people that the republic was a success, then well and good. But if he should fail, then again he would be the exile, and this time with the contumely of the people upon him.

Many a leader, in Sun's place would not have gone to Nanking, except as a passing yet honored guest. Such a leader would have tried to avoid the presidential offer with a humorous evasion: "Gentlemen, don't you think I have done my share? Now please let me sit by and watch you do yours. I have been exiled from China for a long time and should like to enjoy the home-coming. I really am not prepared for such serious business, so let some other man step up and tackle the job where I leave off. For thirty years I have had rather hard work keeping my head on my shoulders. Don't you think it would be better if I watched the success that the rest of you will hopefully achieve?''

It was a tragic moment, a great crisis; and I think that most men would have assumed the rôle of a wit, had they been in Sun's place, rather than the office of an apparently doomed man. For doomed it seemed that Sun would be, with the Son of Heaven still there in the North, holding the scepter of a thousand years over the teeming multitude of China's hosts.

But Sun is made of sterner stuff. It was his duty, and so he went, with Failure whispering over one shoulder, Treachery over the other, and the Giant of Despair athwart his path. Sun never told me much of those momentous three months as the first President of the Republic of China. His mind was so preoccupied with the sole idea of holding the republic together that the mere details of what was done (and, better, what was not done) had escaped his mind as of petty importance compared with the great labor of launching the Chinese ship of state. It was a terrific task for a man even of his experience, but he accomplished the seemingly impossible.

On December 29, 1911, Sun was elected President of the Republic of China by the convention at Nanking and entered the great walls of the Republic's capital on the afternoon of the

Christian New Year of 1912. Before the sun had set on that day he had taken the oath of office and assumed the responsibility for the continuance of the republic which he had created. Cannon were booming, fireworks bursting, and great lanterns made an avenue of light, such as Nangking, the city of a hundred ages, never had known before; but over all there hung the gloom of uncertainty, and a great cloud of doubt of what the morrow should bring forth.

In his inaugural address, the first President of the Chinese Republic reiterated his pledge to democracy. His words were brief, and the eloquence of his voice took on the tone of a judge announcing the verdict of a jury.

Then the momentous days rolled along, each hour of which was a suspense such as the patriotic ringer of the American Liberty Bell felt, as, with the rope in his hands, he waited doubtfully, hour after hour, for the summons to strike out the tidings. China was a republic, but the influence of its new liberty did not extend its benefits over the Chinese of all China. There was still another liberty bell to ring, and many doubting Thomases declared that the second tidings of liberty would never be heard.

However, on the twenty-fifth day of the twelfth moon of the third year of Hsuang Tung (February 12, 1912), the second liberty bell did ring; the second tidings came with the decree of Manchu abdication. At last the full success of Chinese democracy had been achieved, duty was fulfilled, and now Sun had the right to withdraw as chief magistrate of the nation. Two days after the decree of Manchu abdication Sun addressed the Republican Assembly and tendered his resignation.

"The North and the South are brought together by the abdication of the Ching emperor. Yuan promises to—and will, I believe—support the Republic. He is a man of experience in affairs of state, and a loyal supporter of that democracy for which we have so long labored. I can serve my country as well in administrative work. Let Yuan become President in my stead. He promises to serve the people of the Republic."

Such was the sense of the message with which Sun put before the members of his Parliament, well knowing that they would do as he wished.

February 15, 1912, in conformance, and upon the recommendation of Sun, Yuan Shih Kai was elected Sun's successor. On March 1, Sun gave to Yuan the chief magistracy of the Chinese Republic. Sun had held the Republic together because he was the soul of honor, moderate in his power, and firm for democracy. Sun believed that he had in Yuan a man of his own qualities. Sun the Forgiving, with the credulity that goes with goodness, gave his staff and his mantle to Yuan, never dreaming that Yuan would prove his Judas and become a tyrannical monster opposing the advance of the people.

Thus Sun the Magnanimous delivers the red bag, with his magisterial seal of office, to Yuan; and now, from the yellow scroll, is heard the eulogies which, by resolution of the Assembly, voice the feeling of the Chinese people toward the Founder of the Republic. Alas! Yuan the Red was to make the blood of Chinese patriots run redder than the red of that bag, nor was there a use of that seal that Yuan was not to blot with human blood; but the eulogies of Sun Yat Sen inscribed on that yellow scroll are still heard, mellowing with time.

## XXXIV

IT IS accepted as a matter of Chinese history
that Sun was *tricked* out of the presidency by
Yuan, who made Sun believe that he, Sun, could
do a greater work in improving the economic
condition of China as its railroad builder and
director rather than by giving up his whole day's
work to listening to the supplications of office-
seekers and franchise-grabbers. In the long days
I spent with Sun I never heard him complain
about Yuan's getting the presidency away from
him, although he did express himself as regret-
ting the misfortune that befell the Chinese people
in Yuan's usurpation of the presidency. Sun is
a planter rather than a gleaner. All his life long
he has been like a farmer who plants in the raw
springtime to give his friends the pleasure of
gathering the easy harvest of the pleasant summer. Sun thought that Yuan was a friend of the
Chinese people. So why not? Liberty-loving

304

Yuan could take care of the presidency (a slow and over-formal job for a man of Sun's temperament), and Sun could thus get down among the people and stir them up into the new economic ideas for which he had formed the Republic. So out goes President Sun, the guileless, and in goes the Traitor Yuan, the cunning.

After his resignation on March 1, 1912, Sun went to Wuchang for the development of his railroad plans, and thence to Canton and other centers of China; then in August he went to Peking to consider further railroad development with Yuan. Yuan welcomed Sun regally and treated him with the greatest honors, establishing an elaborate residence for him in the Foreign Office building. It may interest some to know that Sun's special quarters were established in the great reception-room known as the Shi Jen Foo Tung. Yuan conferred with Sun constantly during the months Sun remained in Peking. Yuan agreed with everything that Sun proposed. Sun offered no program of interference but was insistent upon plans of political and economic reconstruction. In all these plans Yuan showed but a mild interest actually, although he pretended cunningly to be greatly interested. Finally Sun discovered that Yuan was not a man of modern ideas; hence, he no longer wondered why Yuan did not ask questions and did not enter into serious study of the rebuilding of China. Although the discussion covered a great field, Yuan merely acceded to all that Sun said. Sun's suspicions would have been awakened in this ever-acquiescent attitude of Yuan, had he been a man of more suspicious character. As it was, he was surprised, but not to the point of suspicion. Yuan's lack of interest in the plans came, he presumed, not from an inner disregard but rather because the subject was new to Yuan. But Sun was not yet willing to admit that Yuan was an old, tricky official who would never show any regard for the good of China. In the conferences held, every once in a while, Yuan would break out into the most violent abuse of the old dynasty and would praise unstintingly the effect of the Revolution. It was all very melodramatic, but Sun Yat Sen the unsuspecting was too concentrated in his devotion to his country's needs even to laugh at Yuan's play for his regard in this behalf.

All the long years that Sun, with a price on his head, was building up his revolution, Yuan was being coddled in the warm lap of Manchu luxury. It seemed very rich humor, Yuan's vituperation of the Imperialist hand that had fed him all those years and which he was the last to kiss. But on the theory that bygones are bygones, Sun Yat

Sen merely smiled indulgently at Yuan's protestations as to how he had been cunningly victimized by the Manchus. Sun's aim was to get China started on the road of progress, not to dig up the buried unpleasantness of the past. The conduct of Yuan was in keeping with his general character, to revile when he thought it popular and praise when it brought him popularity. But even when Yuan became, in the judgment of Sun, a truckling opportunist whose only schooling had been obtained through his boot-licking adherence to the Manchus (who had made much of Yuan's uncle, Li Hung Chang), Sun was not afraid of Yuan's influence. Sun believed that China was now thoroughly awakened to the task before her and that the Chinese would brush everything aside to develop their modernity along the path of progress which he had mapped out for them. He did not see how Yuan could really do any harm in his attempts to aggrandize himself. It seemed to Sun that by the very effect of his own voluntary resignation from the presidency, and the obligation which he had thus imposed upon Yuan by the conditions of his resignation, Yuan would be surrounded by a wall of restraint which his apparently clumsy ambition would never be able to vault. Yuan was, inwardly, much as his appearance was outwardly. Corpulent from lack of exercise and from overindulgence of his appetite, he was lazy, even in his speech, and his cumbrous knock-kneed personality did not offer anything that suggested the swiftness of cunning action that his brain eventually disclosed.

The circumstances that protected the people against all political trickery seemed to Sun's mind to lie in the condition of the minds of the Chinese people. He believed that now they were thoroughly awake. He had labored for so many years to achieve the triumph that had at last come to him that in the enthusiasm of his almost fully accomplished victory he would not believe that any obstacle could now be put in the way of the further triumph of the Chinese people. During the quarter of a century and more that he had crusaded about the world in furtherance of the plan to found the republic, he felt that he had through his wide-spread secret organizations formed such an intimate acquaintance with the Chinese people that he could read the slightest alteration in their thought. He knew that this thought had come entirely to favor the republic, and that now even the old reverence for the throne of the Son of Heaven was gone forever. He felt that the people would brook no interference with their forward plan, and that if Yuan Shih Kai failed at any time to stand by the republic founded

by the people the masses would rise in their
wrath and thrust him aside. He had seen how
the army of Yuan had thrown down their arms
to join the cause of the revolution. Sun Yat Sen
knew that this was not the doing of Yuan but
rather of the soldiers themselves, who added their
armed support to the movement of the people.

One thing greatly distressed Sun. Yuan, in
the appointment of incumbents to new and old
offices, did not pay any attention to the fitness of
the men whom he was appointing, and who were
ostensibly to carry on the reconstruction work of
the Republic; but if the men were merely honest
who were thus appointed by Yuan, Sun did not
feel that he had reason to object. To make a
charge of dishonesty against an appointee involved questions of fact which it would take some
time to determine. Perhaps they had been corrupt
under the old régime when everything was rotten
and every one corrupt, and still they might be able
under the stimulus of the new order to serve as
honest officials. Sun, however, brought the matter
of the appointments to a direct issue. Yuan
suavely responded:

"What is your wish in regard to the distribu-
tion of the posts of the central government?"

"What I want," declared Sun, "is, first of all,
honest officials. But China needs more virtues

from its officials than honesty. China needs officials who have the ability to create those new conditions that will make Chinese prefer to go into industrial pursuits to make money rather than to hold office for the purpose of money-grafting. I care nothing about who is named an officer under the Central Government,'' asserted Sun, ''as long as the people themselves are allowed full opportunity through their legal representations to name them without restriction. I do not care to put any of my friends in office, because I do not wish to conflict in any way with the work of the executive control from which I have resigned. My work is now constructive. I do not wish to interfere in even the remotest way with your free conduct of office. Should I not allow you free use of your office, then the responsibility for any failures would fall upon me in proportion to my interference. I do not wish to interfere in *your* executive work, and do not wish that any one should interfere in *my* constructive work. Should I make a personal appointment of one of my friends, then I place myself under obligations to you. Hence, I myself care for no patronage of office. It is my desire to commence as speedily as possibly my constructive work, and in this behalf I shall commence with the organization of the railroad system which

I contemplate for China. Once we have a railroad system fully developed in China, then we
shall open up avenues of trade and commerce
for the welfare of the people. Agricultural China
will become also an industrial China. Men who
now seek public office because of the lure of the
'squeeze' will then turn aside from trying to get
rich out of the money collected from the people
as taxes, and work in the newer and more lucrative fields of employment."

"And how can you do all this?" asked Yuan,
his dull yet cunning interest at last rather
awakened. Anything that would relieve the
public treasury from the pillage of his harpies
appealed to him. By driving off the harpies, or
by finding other employment for them, cunning
Yuan knew that he would have all the more spoils
left for himself.

"Railways, first of all, are necessary to develop
new fields of endeavor," responded Sun. "A
private institution for the building of these railways operating under the Republic should be
created by the Parliament of the Chinese Republic. This will be somewhat in accordance with the
American plan of building railroads. If the roads
are owned by the Government, then they will be
subjected to the importunities of office-seekers.
If they are owned by private corporations or

311

groups of private companies, they will not be able to make liberal loans abroad, because of their private character. If, however, they are private organizations, and still controlled by the Government, then they will be free from politics and still have the benefit of government control."

To this Yuan acceded. He was willing to promise anything to make Sun believe that he was the friend of the people. He thought with complacency how he had duped the founder of the republic; that republic of which he was on October 6, 1913, to elect himself President for life, in such wise that the method of election made the office hereditary in his own family, paving the way for the ultimate declaration by which he proclaimed himself emperor and successor to the Son of Heaven. But Yuan's way of wickedness was not altogether lined with roses. Space does not allow much further comment upon Yuan in his treachery toward Sun; but I think that at all events I should briefly speak of Yuan's "Backyard Murder of General Chang."

On August 15, 1912, General Chang Chen Wu, with the surrender of his own life as the victim of a foul and senseless murder, played the principal part in a bloody tragedy that showed how desperately forlorn the Government of China was becoming under the tyranny of Yuan Shih Kai.

Chang, a native of Huping, became soldier by profession. He was an adherent of the Sun Yat Sen group, and the uprising at Wuchang made him a general. During the terrific military action at Wuchang in 1912, a Manchu general, Li Huan Yang, who as a brigadier-general was in command at Wuchang, in order to save his own pelt, turned against the Manchus and joined the Revolutionists. The story current (true generally, details uncertain) concerning the way Li finally was induced to join the republican ranks is as follows:

General Chang, who was of a plucky fearless type, bravely sought out General Li with a company of picked soldiers. General Li ran about from one chamber of his quarters to the other and finally found refuge under a bed. Chang stormed through the building from corner to corner, and finally saw Li's heels just showing under the bed, where Li lay face downward, prostrated by fear. "Advance!" commanded General Chang to his soldiers. The room was soon packed with Chang's seasoned soldiers, who ranged themselves under orders about the room, so that at a single additional command their volley would blow Li to the ceiling. Silence prevailed, while the soldiers watched their general saunter up in a nonchalant Chinese fashion, very ceremoniously to where the pair of heels were sticking out from beneath the bed. Even more ceremoniously, General Chang reached down and, grabbing the pair of heels in a firm grip, gave a quick pull, and out on the floor lay the terrified General Li. General Chang assisted him to rise, expressed great solicitude for General Li's health, and then quietly asked:

"General Li, we shall be greatly honored if you and your entire brigade immediately join our Republican ranks. Do you accept our invitation?"

"Most heartily," responded General Li. "The honor is mine, not yours." In this picturesque and intensely "Chinesy" way, General Li became the subordinate of General Chang, with his entire brigade in all the bloody revolutionary work that followed.

Was it any wonder that General Li from that time on, hated Chang and wished to bring about his destruction? It took Li a long time to obtain his revenge, but obtain it he eventually did.

General Li had great influence with Yuan Shih Kai; so Li induced Yuan to invite General Chang to come up as an honored guest at Peking "to talk over affairs of government." Flowery, indeed, was the language of the invitation. Chang was delighted to be thus honored and went up immediately to Peking. Yuan gave him a great feast of welcome. Chang was happy in the honor of the welcome and gratified with the generosity of the hospitality. Then came Yuan's command.

"To death with him!"

So the detachment of soldiers who had been detailed for that purpose even before the feasting began took General Chang back into the quiet of the garden and murdered him forthwith.

It was a quiet little affair at the time; merely a matter of friendly accommodation on the part of Yuan the Red toward his good friend, Li the Treacherous; anything to accommodate a friend; and, moreover, Yuan himself did not care much for Chang, and hence, in murdering Chang, he was killing two birds with one stone. Official murders were the order of the day during Yuan's bloody reign, and Yuan thought that this quiet and convenient little murder would soon "blow over" like the others.

In this, however, Yuan made a great mistake, for hardly was General Chang's dead body cold before the wrath of certain of Chang's friends commenced to show itself; and, through the protests of these friends, finally the people, hearing of the foul deed, commenced to murmur at the most unprovoked and deliberate murder. So notorious had the story of General Chang's murder become that at last it served Yuan's increasing list of enemies as something tangible; something upon which they could join, regardless of other interests, in their secret campaign against Yuan the Red. Yuan at first laughed, then became serious, and finally began to tremble; for he feared that after all some successful attempt might be made upon his own life, from among the friends of General Chang, instigated by the wrath of the people. Then the Advisory Council denounced Yuan, and Yuan's terror grew; for at that earlier period he had not fully secured his tyrannical position so that he could loiter idly in the debauchery of his harem among his concubines in the enjoyment of the wine-cup and the opium-pipe. Indeed, he was sore beset with new fears that continually obsessed him as he sought surcease on the opium-couch. In his dreams he could hear the increasing murmurs of the people. Who would come to his aid? Who would silence the voices that were rising in protest against him? Ah! there was just one man to save him from the wrath of the people. "If Sun Yat Sen comes, he will save me," reflected Yuan.

So he sent a prayerful invitation to Sun Yat Sen to come to Peking and be the guest of the nation.

"Do not go," urged Sun's followers. "He

only invites thee to slay thee, as he did General Chang."

"It is my duty to go," declared Sun. "Over this foul murder of Chang, by an estrangement in republican ranks, civil war may ensue. We must have the unity of the Chinese Republic preserved. If I do not go to Peking, the people will think that I am afraid of Yuan. If I do go, the people will know that I am there to protect their interests and not to defend this wicked murder."

So Sun proceeded to Peking immediately.

Yuan sent the Son of Heaven's chariot to bring Sun from the Peking railway station to the palace. Whole regiments of Yuan's picked soldiery attended the Founder of the Chinese Republic, and all Peking turned out to do him honor. Never in that ancient seat of Manchu imperial control was there a more real or affectionate welcome given by the people. After the second day, however, Sun refused to use the imperial chariot and, furthermore, ordered that his retinue of soldiers be cut down to one hundred men, the usual Chinese guard of honor.

I asked Sun, "Were you not afraid that the predictions of your followers would come true, and that you, too, would be murdered by Yuan?"

Sun smiled.

"No, because I knew that Yuan was a very

cautious man, and I knew that he would not dare
to take my life, since he feared reprisals from my
supporters.''

Sun the Sympathetic found Yuan in a state of
abject repentance; or, at least, repentance it
seemed to Sun the Susceptible. Almost the first
words after the greetings were over were expressed most bitterly.

''Why did you take Chang's life?'' demanded
Sun, acrimoniously. Yuan cringed, and then
weakly answered:

''Because Li sent me a telegram saying that
Chang was plotting, not only against Li, but also
against the Government.'' (By Government, of
course, Yuan meant himself.) ''Therefore, since
he was plotting against the Government, it seemed
that he should be executed.''

''Wretched man,'' declared Sun, ''do you believe that your fear could justify such an act?''

Then Yuan seemed to show real contrition.
After a while Sun began to feel sorry for him.
Yuan was a rag in his fear; perhaps it was not
remorse, and perhaps it was not penitence—but
something of the sort, at least, it seemed.

Sun continued to upbraid Yuan for his conduct
in having procured the death of Chang. Yuan
continued to express great regret and to defend
himself upon the ground that the urgency of the

telegram demanded quick action in order to prevent another uprising. Yuan's penitence waxed apace. Undoubtedly he was sorry that he had taken the life of Chang. He was sorry because he saw the danger into which his crime had brought him.

Sun remained in Peking a month. A score of times Yuan confided to Sun his troubles and the difficulty that he had to get the support of the people. Finally, Sun realized that if he did not help Yuan the country would be plunged into another civil war. To make popular government secure, it seemed the plain duty of Sun to support Yuan in his extremity. Yuan's crime was most reprehensible, but there were two evils presented; it was plainly Sun's duty to accept the lesser and to pass over the further denunciation of the terrible murder, in an attempt to avoid more bloodshed in civil warfare.

Sun had been called to Peking, not only as a judge of the conduct of Yuan, but as the recognized leader of the people. His duty was toward the people, and the prime duty of all was to avoid civil warfare. There was also some evidence that Yuan really believed himself to be confronted with a bloody uprising, and that, consequently, as a defensive act, in nipping the rebellion in the bud, the execution of Chang was not without some ancient Chinese argument of justification. At all events, the case against Yuan had not been proved beyond a reasonable doubt, and it was Sun's duty, as it seemed at the time, to resolve the doubt in favor of Yuan. So Sun did not denounce Yuan before the whole people and drive him forth from the office that he had disgraced, because China was not in a position to entertain thoughts of civil war. The lot of the poor was already hard. Besides, civil war would stop all progress in China, and Sun's work of construction would have to cease.

There are few triumphs of leadership that can be compared to the recall of Sun to Peking. The people forgave Yuan because their great popular leader declared that Yuan should be forgiven.

Alas, how greatly Sun was to regret this act of forgiveness.

# EIGHTH PERIOD

October 27, 1913, to Yuan's death, June 6, 1916

Post-Presidential Exile

## XXXV

EXILE UNDER YUAN SHIH KAI'S RÉGIME—DIRECTION OF
THE "PUNISH-YUAN EXPEDITION"—THE GUNBOAT
DRAMA OF THE WHANG PO—THE LAST WICKEDNESS
OF YUAN THE RED.

WHEN Sun forgave Yuan at Peking for the
foul murder of Chang, he believed that
Yuan would make good his promise to mend his
way. In this belief, however, Sun was soon to be
deceived. It would take a book larger than this
to tell the tale of China's sorrows under the
tyranny of Yuan the Red. Suffice it to say that
when Yuan's Parliament met for the last time
on April 9, 1913, Sun Yat Sen sent Yuan this
message:

"You have been a traitor to your country. As
I rose against the Manchu Emperor, so, also, shall
I rise against you."

By this time, however, Yuan had a great disciplined army to support him in his tyranny, but,
notwithstanding this army, Sun commenced another revolution, this time against Yuan, which,
from July, 1913, he waged against terrible odds

until August 27, 1913, when, after the bloody battle of Nanking, he was compelled again to establish his headquarters in Japan, this time a refugee from the bloody hand of Yuan the Red. Sun, however, undaunted by Yuan's large army and great treasure, organized anew his old revolutionary forces, this time against Yuan. This anti-Yuan revolution was winning full success when the reason for its existence ceased with the death of Yuan at Peking, June 6, 1916. It may be interesting to review the events of this period, which, for lack of space, we shall pass over quickly.

In September, 1913, after the second revolution had broken out with the "Punish-Yuan Expedition," Sun Yat Sen was asked by the Shanghai Consular Body to leave Shanghai. Dr. Sun had not come to Shanghai with any idea of finding a refuge there. He had come to Shanghai for his work in connection with the Chinese National Railroad Administration. It was several days before he could comply with the request of the Shanghai Consular Body, finally taking passage on a German ship, his purpose being to go to Canton to direct the fight against Yuan. On this trip, however, the German steamer called at the port of Foochow, ninety miles up the Min River, and with the landing and delivery of cargo considerable delay in the voyage to Canton was involved. Hence it was that he was too late to direct the battle at Canton, in which the Cantonese soldiers were beaten and dispersed, Governor-General Chen Kwing Ming having fled from Canton to Singapore. Complications increased by reason of the fact that Sun's arrest was ordered in Hong Kong. Accordingly, he transhipped at Foochow to a Japanese cargo-ship, which took him to Formosa, the Japanese consul having arranged his passport for the changed voyage. Arriving at Formosa, he changed to another Japanese steamer, which took him to Moji in Japan, and thence he proceeded to Tokyo. I give in something of detail the way Sun left China in this "Punish-Yuan" war, because, as will be noted, it shows that Providence shaped his course so that he was compelled to leave China. Having been, by Providence, as it were, settled in Japan, he made that land his headquarters to direct operations against Yuan. It was a very disheartening period for Sun; for many of his leading supporters were now becoming discouraged, declaring that China had always been under the rule of a tyrant and that it was impossible to obviate tyrannical rule. One of his

325

leading supporters, Yuan Wang Ching, one day expressed his discouragement, whereupon Sun, after listening most sympathetically, replied:

"Why do you despair? Why do you lament? For ten years we labored without any success whatsoever. Then we had success. Now comes failure again, so let us forget the success and go back to where we left off ten years before."

He knew that his followers thought with the overthrow of the Imperialists he had achieved a complete success and that, therefore, their discouragement was great at the failure to maintain this success. Hence, he had to enhearten them by making them feel that all success was more or less comparative.

Although defeated, he knew that his position was better than it had been three years before. For now the actual success of the reform movement showed the people what could be done. Therefore, greater confidence from the people could be expected for the future, for the people would be more and more willing to take part in the movement and bring about the betterment of China.

Some of his followers, however, did not agree with Sun, and hence, unfortunately, there grew up a division in the revolutionary movement. Some declared that they were conformists and that they would go no further in view of the failure, since, to them in their discouragement, it seemed impossible to achieve success a second time. Others, however, believed that the opportunity was still before them. From among the strong-hearted of his following he built up a new revolutionary society with Tokyo as a center of its deliberations. In this new society he instituted a stronger discipline than ever before. Every follower was made to understand that he must follow the order of the party.

I shall attempt to give an idea of the methods used by Sun against Yuan Shih Kai by telling the story of the Gunboat Drama of the Whangpo.

Dr. Sun's funds were not sufficient for a strong military movement against Yuan, and even if this had been possible such a movement might be overcome by the intervention of certain foreigners who were, for their own selfish purposes, allied with Yuan. To give battle against Yuan in the open field would involve the immediate chance of a defeat from the overwhelming numerical superiority of Yuan's soldiery. Something else had to be done. Sun therefore decided upon staging a dramatic protest in a Dare-to-Die movement against the wickedness of Yuan.

The harbor of Shanghai on the Whangpo is the busiest center of all China and one of the greatest ports of the whole world. Sun, therefore, decided that the *mise en scène* for this Dare-to-Die protest was to be in the waters of the Whangpo. It was the sort of movement that the Dare-to-Dies delight in. It was a movement of great danger, however, on the part of only a few of Sun's followers. Sun could not have selected a better point for this "memorial" against the wickedness of Yuan than in the waters of the harbor of Shanghai. As above noted, not only is Shanghai the greatest emporium of the Far East, but as a center of political intelligence it has world-reaching advantages. All the important nations of the globe are represented here, not only by consulates, but by active business and commercial agencies that are quick to respond to the mutations of Chinese politics.

The broad sweep of the Whangpo, the River of the Yellow Quays, widening out in a deep channel over a score of miles from the Yangtze, is crowded with the ships of war and commerce of all nations, which come and go with the flow and ebb of every tide. Under the frowning guns of the warcraft and the huge chimneys of the transpacific and Suez liners, the bat-winged junks of the far-off gorges of the upper Yangtze mingle with fishing-craft of the China Sea. It is a great *mise en scène;* no scenery more thrilling for this

DR. AND MRS. SUN
Taken about the time of his marriage in Japan on October 25, 1915
(Page 355).

"Sun does, indeed, have a most magnetic gaze, particularly when his eyes kindle up in a great glow and stare out like a lion" (Page 245).

protest of the Founder of the Chinese Republic against the rule of a tyrant. Yonder is the proud line of lofty banking concerns and great houses of commerce, and here the tall flagstaffs floating banners of defiance over the consulates of the leading nations of the world. It is a foreign scene and might be transplanted to New York or London, for in all this show of power it is the foreigner, the Ocean-man, who is the central figure; and even the monstrous rule of Yuan the Red does not affect the political life of the Ocean-man as he complacently wends his way on the Bund, under the noses of his frowning gun-boats.

This battle drama will not be a great one either as regards the number of actors or the actual physical effect of attempted destruction; but in the thrill of its incentive, in the emotion of its assembling, and in the justice of its purpose, it has the spirit of Thermopylæ and the heart-throb of the Alamo.

Yuan had two gunboats in the waters of the Whangpo, just below Shanghai's broad streets. Sun's plan was to take one of these boats and then use it to overcome the other one. No very great physical success was expected to come from this movement, for the gunboats, when taken by Sun's followers, would have to make off for sea, and probably not be able to do much in support of

329

any military or naval movement contemplated later on. But Sun felt satisfied that the plan he had conceived, that of capturing a gunboat in the midst of the foreign shipping of Shanghai, would produce the effect of awaking the lethargic Chinese element to the necessity for action against the now openly declared imperial policy of Yuan.

The revolutionist attack on Yuan's gunboat was successfully made, and Sun's Dare-to-Dies were soon in possession of it from bow to stern, having taken all on board as prisoners.

Having effected the capture of the gunboat with small loss of life, Sun's men then proceeded to attempt to carry out the rest of the program by forcing the surrender of the other gunboat through the use of the cannon on the one which they had already captured. All would have gone well, had it not been for the lightning-action of the Chinese keeper of the ammunition on the captured Yuan Shih Kai boat. The Dare-to-Dies, having possessed themselves of the guns, demanded surrender of the keys to open the door of the ammunition-chamber, for to use the cannon to capture the other boat the cannon had to be loaded. A flash through the air was the answer to this command, the ammunition keeper having thrown overboard the key to the iron ammunition-compartment. Even against the fire from the opposing gunboat, however, Sun's men held their positions until the survivors were ready to retire to the shore.

This incident, trivial as it was in actual effect, did not turn out to be the fiasco that Sun's enemies declared it was, for it served as a dramatic protest against Yuan's tyranny. It was the Chinese way of doing things, but, in the Chinese way, it was effective.

In the hope that the little drama of the gunboats of Whangpo may serve to illustrate something of the actual protest continually made by Sun against Yuan Shih Kai, we shall hurry on to bring this period to a close.

Yuan caused himself to be proclaimed Emperor of China on December 3, 1915, and for the next six months China was literally under a reign of terror. One of the last savage acts of the demon Yuan the Red, according to the terrified talk of Peking's streets and tea-houses, was to rush, maddened at the thought that his wicked power was drawing to a close, into the bedchamber of one of his girl-concubines. Upon this poor girl he sprang, venting his angry spleen against the world by slashing her with his sword and, at the same time, destroying the babe which she had faithfully borne him, finally going back to his chambers, dripping with the blood of the dead mother and of his and her babe. Does not Yuan Shih Kai well deserve the name of Yuan the Red?

Even the wickedness of Yuan the Red, however, had to come to an end. On June 6, 1916, almost six months to the day from the date of his self-coronation as Emperor of China, Yuan died—some say by poison; some, from dissipation; but all, from Providence's kindest dispensation. Yes, Providence had at length removed Yuan the Red, Sun's archenemy. New hope and courage now possessed the followers of Sun Yat Sen.

## NINTH PERIOD

From Yuan's death, June 6, 1916, to the present, with something of the Reformer's life at Shanghai, 1918-21.

### READJUSTMENT

## XXXVI

**P**ATRIOTIC Chinese hoped for great things
after Yuan's death on June 6, 1916. I regret that this series of episodic chapters will not
permit a review of Sun Yat Sen's activities in
behalf of these patriotic hopes from the date of
Yuan's death down to the present time. Although space does not permit this, it will permit
relating something that he did not do, an omission which I believe to have been a most serious
mistake. In his omission he was logical and consistent; as to its effect I shall leave the reader to
judge.

I had always considered that Sun Yat Sen
should take advantage of extending Chinese democratic propaganda to America, the sister republic across the seas. Shortly after the Great
War, when China, in commerce, had been brought
economically nearer to America than ever before,
I believed that Sun with his eloquence had a clear
chance to obtain support in America. In 1919
Chinese-American trade was booming, passenger

ships had their waiting lists booked up months ahead, and there was a friendly attitude toward the republic that Sun had founded, widely and openly expressed in America. The emotions of the Great War had spread out over the Pacific in something of a protest against tuchun (military despot) militarism. At last American thinkers interested in China were realizing that Sun, in spite of his protest against China's entry into the great War, was the prophet of the Chinese people in an attempt to overcome the militarists of Peking. Moreover things were going from bad to worse in Peking. A great American bank had been flatly denied even the interest on a huge loan made to the Peking militarists, and the American capitalists, who had thought to increase their investments in China, now wondered if it would not be best to support the actual republic rather than the *tuchun* dummy that had been rigged up in Peking. Then, again, popular sentiment in America was at that time peculiarly favorable to Sun and his party, for he had been in discreet retirement long enough to awaken a new interest in his whereabouts. Sun's Kuo Ming Tong (Nationalist) party in America had prospered through the great prosperity of its members, and, since nothing succeeds like success, Americans who patronized Chinese restaurants, shops, and laundries found a new regard for the Chinese in their progress and prosperity abroad.

Having published a magazine for Dr. Sun's party, I was in a position, perhaps, to know well the favorable psychological situation that existed the year following the Great War between the American and the Chinese minds as expressed through Sun and his Kuo Ming Tong. It was the period of the making and the unmaking of nations and the most favorable hour in Sun's long struggle to obtain recognition from America. I felt that if I could get Sun to take the stump in America before great American audiences he would work up a sentiment in his favor which would give him overwhelming support, and which eventually would restore him to the complete control of China.

In trying to devise ways and means, I had canvassed the situation among influential American friends in the banking, commercial, and political world, many of whom I had known from my boyhood. Without exception, they listened to me with great interest, but to a man all declared that the situation was too new for them to give any suggestions of value about it. Most of them agreed, however, that the only way to handle a campaigning tour of this nature would be through the Chautauqua. There was also some advice as to obtaining a "rider" in the political platform of a certain prominent American party, in order to focus public attention in America upon Sun Yat Sen. Although none of my American friends could give me any helpful suggestions, the encouragement of their serious attention to the subject greatly enheartened me. Finally, I communicated with certain great Chautauqua agencies, with the result that I had princely offers in the event I could contract for the speaking services of Sun Yat Sen; in fact, one of the Chautauqua offers from a very responsible institution was practically to the effect that they would pay anything demanded for a series of lectures.

The matter was rather long drawn out, and the final offer came to me by cablegram in China. Armed with my facts and figures and the formal offers, after some further consideration I finally concluded to broach the matter to Sun immediately and even abruptly.

"Doctor, there is a great opportunity waiting for you in America," I began; and with these words I passed over to him the cablegrams and other papers connected with the offers I had received, together with a detailed sketch of the method of propaganda and press work that was to go with it. I had all the details as I thought

338

down to a nicety, even to the schedule of the steamers and railroads, and I smiled complacently as I showed him the balance-sheet indicating the large rewards over and above all expenses.

The doctor thought a long time and glanced over the cables and papers in an absent-minded way. He remained deep in reverie for some moments and then said, as though speaking to himself:

"I would, indeed, like to greet the American people. What a pleasant trip it would be!"

Encouraged by this remark, I put forth my argument. His health had not been good during the beginning of the winter of 1919-20, and the trip would fortify him. He had been under a strain for years, and this friendly voyage—greeting the new friends to be found in America—would have a recreative effect. Besides, although *tuchun* politics was very active in China, there was a lull in militarism which could be taken advantage of.

"Ah!" exclaimed the doctor at the last argument, "that's just the reason that I think I should not go. My duty—does it not seem to be right here? I can't tell what might happen while I am away."

He sighed, and the light in his face faded into

an expression of resignation. A deep sympathy possessed me. I knew that Sun wanted to go to America very much. He had never had a vacation in his whole life; he was beginning to show the strain of his years of toil. This holiday—something that he wanted so much—was tendered him on a golden platter. The Canadian *Empress* steamer had just been put on the Shanghai run, and after two weeks of luxurious travel he would be in invigorating America with multitudes of new-found friends to greet him. No more worrying over *tuchuns;* no more daily precaution against their machinations to overthrow his work; free from care in the land of happiness and friendship—there it was, all before him, together with a substantial amount of money to turn over for the furtherance of his work or to do what he wished with. I pleaded with him for half an hour. Finally he seemed to yield to this offer of a surcease from his labor and said quietly and with a smile that I believed to forecast his acceptance:

"We shall talk it over the next time you come."

I left the cablegrams and papers with him, convinced that he would accept the offer. That night he became ill; in fact, he was ill when he got up to receive me that very day. It was some time before I saw him.

340

He was sitting in his library and was dressed in his military suit of gray worsted, as usual without insignia of any kind.

"Good, Doctor!" I exclaimed. "I see that you have your field-suit on. I presume this is a sign that you are going to America." He smiled, picked up the cablegrams and papers, and looked them over wistfully.

"It was good of you to go to all this trouble," he said in even a lower voice than usual. (When Sun expressed gratitude, he always spoke low, as though he wished the beating of his heart to join in the expression.) He looked out of the wide window and sighed. The day was damp, gloomy, with a breath of clammy air that even the bright glow of the chimney-grate could not disperse. He gazed out at the leafless trees, the withered flower-beds and brown grass of the compounds beyond and sighed again. I do not know whether he saw these dead things of winter, for I went and stood beside him, and he did not seem to notice me. I said nothing more, for I was accustomed to Sun's long periods of silence. I felt satisfied that he had resolved to go with me. Why not? He was still somewhat ill from both overwork and climatic causes. I had convinced him I felt sure that it was worth while to undertake this pleasure trip, leaving the sadly congested conditions of overworked China for the land of plenty, pleasure, and abundance that would be so glad to receive him. Just a brief trip, and then a return to China; for I had now enlarged the proposal so that we could come and go whenever we saw fit. Three weeks, and we should be amid the rose-gardens of Puget Sound or the citrus-groves of California.

"I hope that you have concluded to go on the junket tour," I declared in a facetious attempt, for I felt very jolly over the thought that it was all so easy. "Junks are emblematic of China's heavy burdens, and junkets the symbols of America's abundance; the one needs the other just as you need new relaxation and at least a short change."

Sun came back, picked up the papers, and folded them very carefully and as slowly as the priest closes the great Bible of the altar.

I know that at that moment Sun realized the importance of his decision. Here was the golden hour of opportunity come to him at last. Here was the chance to enter the gate of American public opinion with skilled American advisers to show him the way to America's favor. With their sympathy would come a support that would make *tuchun* militarism tremble. Again Sun would be the full master. Besides, there would be the pleasure of the voyage; the ease and comfort; freedom from care and from those hundreds of importunities with which he allowed himself to be burdened. A vacation at last! Back to America, this time not as an exile but as the guest of a great American public, who would throng in thousands into the great auditoriums and theaters to be thrilled by his eloquence. It was no effort for Sun to address the multitude, and the element of a speaking campaign made the prospect of the trip all the more pleasant. Yes, this was the hour, and America was the place.

"It is difficult to say no," he finally declared, and passed the papers over to me solemnly as a judge giving a reluctant judgment.

"What! You are not going?" I exclaimed in my deep disappointment, and, perhaps, with something of acrimony in my voice. He slowly shook his head and smiled the deep smile of friendship as though forestalling the rebellion which I felt. I softened in a moment, but continued:

"Doctor, you will always be sorry if you do not go. This chance will never come again, for times change, and politics is not like a clock that can be wound up at will. This great political chance will never come again."

He followed me closely, and, seeing his interest

343

newly awakened, like an advocate pleading with a judge for rehearing of a lost case I still kept on:

"Yes, this opportunity will never come again. They will always want to hear you lecture in America, but in a few months the audiences interested in the issue of militarism as a topic of to-day will no longer be there to hear you, for militarism is being forgotten. America fought and helped win the World War upon one single issue, the issue of militarism. America is still interested in that issue. We are technically still at war with Germany, but full treaty peace will come shortly. In a few months the emotion of to-day will cease. America's wounds will be healed and her losses forgotten. There is only one issue upon which you can get the support that you are entitled to in America, and that is the issue of *tuchun* militarism. Yes, in a few months, America will forget that there has ever been such an institution as militarism. It took a great and expensive propaganda to work the American people up to a feeling that kaiserism should be attacked. Now that the cause of the war has been removed, America will follow in the new and pleasanter channels of politics and will have no time to bother about the unpleasant and little known subject of the *tuchuns*."

Again silence for a long time.

"My duty is here. It was good of you to go to all this trouble . . . but I cannot go now. . . ."

I realized that further argument was useless; likewise I had to admit that his refusal to electioneer for China in America was consistent with his insurmountable modesty and his devotion to the Chinese. He did not care to stand in the spotlight overseas when he could still labor on for China in China.

## XXXVII

IT IS natural for the man from the West to consider that the great game of Chinese politics
is played with instruments of treachery, decep-
tion, and death. Conspiracies are common, according to this belief, and assassinations are
supposed to be of frequent occurrence. There is
some truth in this as applied to certain *tuchuns*
of China, but as regards Sun such allegations are
entirely false. When Sun had been proclaimed
President at Nanking and had a well-equipped
army under his control, he did not put his enemies to death. He forgave them; he even gave
some of them posts of honor. Rule by bloodshed
is not a part of the Sun Yat Sen program. His
enemies, however, go to ridiculous extremes in
attempting, through the privilege of court pro-
cedure, to blacken his reputation in this regard.
I have been concerned as counsel in certain cases
where it was charged that Sun's influence had
brought about deadly assaults, and had even
caused the death itself of his enemies through

346

assassination. None of these false and ridiculous charges, however, has ever in the slightest way been proved. I shall select two of these absurd cases, one in the Shanghai International Mixed Court in China, and the other in the courts of Canada. The following brief extract from the daily press report is from the "Shanghai Mercury," April 29, 1921:

*Alleged Revolutionary Assassination; Wide Spread Political Conspiracy; Former Tuchuns Told Off in Court*

A most startling criminal case has just commenced its hearing in the International Mixed Court in which the alleged attempted murder of General Li, formerly Tuchun of Szechwan Province, is charged against Vong Chi-ming, a former officer in the revolutionary forces. . . . Dih Ze Pah was called: This witness, who wore a suit cut in the high-collared style, declared that in 1917 he was a member of the secretariat department of the extraordinary parliament and that he met Yang Shohtin (one of the accused who has not yet been arrested and who is reported to be in Canton) . . . the two of them commenced to make plans to assassinate Gen. Li, with certain other confederates. The witness declared that his sole purpose in pretending to help them on with their plans was to frustrate them as soon as he had sufficient information to act. . . . Rooms were engaged at the Yip Ping Shang Hotel . . . a watch was set to fire upon General Li as soon as he should make a visit to the hotel, where he was known to come from time to time. A study was made of all the passages of the hotel so that after the commission of the deed escape could be made. . . . Witness declared that his conspirators buoyed up his hope by declaring that when Whang Tsing-wei during the Chin dynasty, made an unsuccessful attempt to assassinate Prince Sah at Peking, he was glorified so that from being a mere scholar he was elevated to the honor of a hero even though he had failed.

WITNESS: They told me that even if we failed to assassinate the General I would become as great as Whang Tsing-wei.

QUESTION: Did you agree to help them?

347

WITNESS: Yes. I agreed to help him because I was a great friend of one of the band and although I knew that it was my duty to advise against it, I knew that Doctor Sun Yat-sen had ordered it done and that it would be useless for me to try to prevent it. And another reason was that if I did not agree to help them they would suspect me and then I would not be able to get any information for General Li. . . .

. . . The case was adjourned for a continued hearing tomorrow afternoon. . . .

Without going into the details of the case as above outlined, suffice it to say that several days were spent in the trial, during all the time of which the innocent accused was held without bail.

"Going pretty hard against us," I said to my client one day. He smiled resignedly as he stood shackled to the arm of the officer with the Sikhs' carbines looming up behind him. It was a rainy day, and the police wagon was late in coming, and I asked the officers to let me drive them all over to the Louza Station, where the prisoner was to be conducted. The officers finally consented, after doubly shackling the accused, who was made to take the seat in front beside me while I drove. How Vong did enjoy that ride, even though his heavy shackles rattled every time he moved his hands! The officers bundled him out at Louza Station, but he waved his shackled hands in a *chin-chin* to me, as they slammed the iron gate behind him and hustled him into prison.

Some time after, I had the pleasure of greeting

him in my law-office; needless to say, he no longer wore shackles, for he had been acquitted, as indicated by the judgment of the court as reported in the "North China Daily News":

> In giving judgment, the Assessor said: The whole of the story of the attempted assassination and conspiracy finally depended upon the story told by Dih Ze-pah, and in view of the fact that all the parties were politicians, or acting for political parties, there were many complexities. The Court had had to look for corroborative evidence directly involving the accused. Such evidence was not forthcoming. No arms were found in the man's possession. Nothing of an incriminating nature, neither arms nor documents, were found in prisoner's luggage. Photos of Dr. Sun Yat-sen were not conclusive evidence. In view of the very serious nature of the charge, the evidence was certainly not strong enough to convict upon. . . .

I advised Vong, upon his acquittal, to leave Shanghai immediately, since he might be arrested again on some other trumped-up charge. But he still stayed around in the anteroom of my offices, waiting day after day, at which I wondered. Then finally he came in all wreathed with smiles, bearing a beautiful shield of silver, engraved with a complimentary inscription. "I am going back now," he declared. Poor chap! He had delayed his return to Shanghai and risked further arrest in order to wait for the making of a present for me.

The Canadian case, likewise, was entirely unfounded, and was due more to the hysteria of war than to other circumstances. During the war

Canada became almost terror-stricken at the thought that almost in her midst there was a large foreign population which, being totally alien both in language and customs, might at any time take the bit in its mouth and rampage in some sort of fury. Accordingly an order in council was finally published against certain elements of these alien populations, in which the Chinese Nationalists were included. The account of the assassination which was the base of the Canadian case herein mentioned is related in the following extract from the "Ottawa Evening Journal" of September 15, 1918, as follows:

. . . The Chinese Nationalist League, whose operations the Federal officials have closely watched for some time, commenced its real activities in Canada in May [1917] last. Dr. Sun Yat Sen, one-time president of China, and leader and master-mind behind the revolution of the Southern provinces against the Chinese Government, which government drew its power and support from the provinces of North China, promoted the movement as an auxiliary to the revolutionary party. . . . Up to a few months ago the work of the League in Canada, while open to suspicion, was free from blood taint or violence, but the visit to the Pacific Coast of Chang, Minister of Education in the Chinese Government, afforded opportunity for the fanatics of the League to strike what a Chinese paper, published in the American Pacific Coast, described as a blow for freedom. . . . One evening after his arrival at Victoria, he left the Empress Hotel to go for a stroll, accompanied by his secretary, the Chinese consul, and several Chinese gentlemen who had called to see him. A member of the League, Chong Wung, shot the Minister, wounded one of the other members of the party, and then, while the police were pursuing him, shot himself. This cold-blooded murder was made the subject of extravagant eulogy in publications supporting the League. Much space was devoted to the life of Chong Wung, who was pictured as a martyr sacrificing his own life on the shrine of liberty. Many hundreds of thousands of dollars have been sent from Canada to China, ostensibly for charitable purposes but, in reality, to assist in Dr. Sun Yat Sen's campaign for the overthrow of the pro-ally Government. The Toronto case is practically the first official step toward wiping the organization out of existence, insofar as Canada is concerned. . . .

An urgent call for my professional services was given me in the midst of these exciting conditions, and I immediately made the long journey to the scene of the trouble. I found at the first hearing of the case against the fifty-two Chinese accused in the Toronto court that the only actual help to be had was at the capital, Ottawa, and not at Toronto, for it was a political rather than a judicial case. Presenting myself in the office of the Dominion officials upon my arriving at Ottawa, I tendered my card.

"Don't trouble yourself to give us your card," responded the official. "We all know you very well. In fact, every letter or telegram that you have written or received since you came here has been photographed," continued the official with a businesslike courtesy.

I prepared a brief of my case, and after this long labor was accomplished under the greatest obstacles I found that I would be misunderstood in using it. The war spirit in Canada had risen to such a sublime pitch that not even the sugges-

351

tion of interference or a criticism of the authorities of the law could be entertained. However, as I went about among the broad-minded Canadian authorities, I felt sure that they would do justice painstakingly and carefully. So I stayed on until finally the order in council was suspended in its effect, the justice which I sought was obtained, and the ridiculous charge dissipated.

## XXXVIII

### DOMESTIC LIFE—AT HOME—RUE MOLIÈRE

SUN YAT SEN was married at the age of twenty to Lu Sze, whose native place was only a few miles from his own village. The marriage was in accordance with the old Chinese custom, which allows the parents the right to marry off their children as they please. Hence, it was not until his marriage that he first saw her, although the two had lived only a few miles apart.

Occupied as he was with his strenuous task of organizing a revolution, and uncertain of his own troubled future, Sun Yat Sen at first balked at the idea of marriage. Then, too, since his trip to Honolulu, he had acquired the Occidental respect for self-determination in the choice of a mate, an idea entirely at variance with the old Chinese custom.

But such is the ingrained Chinese instinct of respect to the parents that all considerations were finally swept away.

353

Three children were born of this marriage: Tsi Sung Sun Fo, who since his graduation from the California Berkeley and Columbia Universities has devoted himself to business; Annie Sun Yen, who died in 1913; and Grace Sun An, who after her education in America took up her residence with her mother in Macao.

Absorbed in his efforts at driving out the Manchus, buffeted by a sea of difficulties, and tossed by circumstances all over the world, Sun Yat Sen was unfortunately unable to give to Lu Sze the attentions which a home-staying Chinese husband could offer. Frequent separations, the perils which beset him, and the uncertainties of his position must have been a trying ordeal to Lu Sze, accustomed as she was to the peace of her Kwangtung home.

But much as she besought him to expose himself less to dangers, the call of his country made him deaf to her entreaties and gradually brought on an estrangement between them.

Finally, after his defeat in the so-called Second Revolution when he sought refuge in Japan, she declined to join him, giving as her reason her desire to attend her aged parents.

Upon his insisting that she join him, she suggested that she choose a concubine for him, according to the Chinese custom. But to this Sun Yat Sen was emphatically opposed, so strongly was he against that wide-spread Chinese evil.

Lu Sze then suggested a separation, and after several disagreements they consented to be divorced.

Sun Yat Sen thus remained in exile, a lonely man, and with no one to preside over his household.

Half a year later he met Miss Chung-ling Soong, the daughter of an old friend and fellow-revolutionist, who had spent most of her girlhood in America and had just then been graduated from Wesleyan College.

The two were drawn together in the common purpose of the revolutionary cause. To her he was, in exile, still the leader of China, the land that both of them loved, and for whose advance they both would give their lives.

Their friendship soon developed into love; several months later they were engaged, and on October 25, 1915, they were married in Japan.

Some idea of the home surrounding of the Great Reformer will be had from the foregoing, which has been very kindly prepared for me by a member of the Sun family. With this statement of the domestic life of Sun Yat Sen, let us visit him at his temporary home in 1919-20 at 29 Rue Molière, in the French Concession in Shanghai, China.

We pass over the beautiful, terraced flower park that surrounds the French Cercle Sportif, where the Rue Molière ends at a picturesque bamboo fence, over which the blossoms of the hedges show their colors. The third door from this pretty nook is where the great leader is sojourning.

It is not a large house, but just the sort of home that a man of Sun's strenuous, simple life would select. There is a reception-room, and, beyond, a wondrously cozy dining-room where I have eaten some of the best meals of my life. One flight up-stairs the great leader has his study and library; two or three bedchambers and a great bath complete this modest but most comfortable home. I must not forget the wonderful verandas that, thrown clear open in the mild weather, become a part of the beautiful garden that lies beyond. Most of the furniture is foreign, but as a sort of compromise between the West and East, Dr. Sun and his wife nearly always wear Chinese clothes, the main exception being when the doctor on cold, winter days puts on a heavy, gray woolen suit cut like a uniform, which gives him a very military and commanding ap-

"Dr. Sun and his wife nearly always wear Chinese clothes. . ." (Page 356). When traveling abroad both wear foreign clothes as shown in Dr. Sun's picture here and elsewhere. In military campaigns the Reformer wears a simple uniform without insignia or decorations.

Showing the development of Dr. Sun's "smile of friendship," taken after a long, hard, steam-hot Shanghai day. Dr. Sun never smiles with his cheeks, but with a naturally suppressed, light contraction of the lip-muscles.

pearance in the easy way he wears it. In the summer-time he wears the Chinese skirt and jacket. Dr. Sun enjoys the summers at Shanghai rather than the winters and in his fresh linens and silks looks so cool and immaculate on even the hottest days that I frequently envy him his free-flowing Chinese garments, comfortable even when the thermometer stands at 95 Fahrenheit, and with 80 per cent humidity and even higher.

The doctor is a careful dietitian, and during meal periods I frequently find benefit in the expert observations which he makes concerning diet and the digestive combinations of foods. He lives a life of extreme abstinence and simplicity, neither smokes nor uses alcohol, and eats most sparingly of the simplest of foods. The table is always beautifully laid and the service noiseless and appetizing. At times I am rather embarrassed at the large number of courses laid at mealtime, since generally the doctor and I are alone, and I know that the dishes have been prepared especially for me. Sometimes the doctor takes, perhaps, only some California tinned peaches with cream, a combination of which he is very fond, though he is sparing in its use. He is even a sparing drinker of tea, a rare denial for a Chinese. We always have a very delicately flavored tea, with a daintily withered Chinese rose-petal or jasmine-leaf to increase its fragrance. I call it, much to the doctor's amusement, the "monkey-tail tea," that being rather more a traditional tea than a real one. The name comes from the ancient tale that the branches of the tea-shrub from which it is fixed are so delicate and tall that monkeys are trained to go up in the willowy branches and gently brush the leaves down with their tails. I asked the doctor where the tea came from, for I drank quantities of it, never really having cared much for tea before. "This is monkey-tail tea, is n't it, doctor?" But the doctor merely responded:

"I'm glad you like it."

When it became known that I was closely identified with the Reformer, I was frequently asked and even importuned by foreigners to take them over and present them to Dr. Sun. I rarely conformed to their requests, but when I did Sun never failed to allow the presentation. On one occasion a splendid old American tourist, who had not been spoiled by large wealth, and who was a man of political influence, prevailed upon me to present him to Sun. He had formed a great admiration for Sun and when presented lost no time in expressing his admiration of the Reformer and in giving him some big-hearted advice as to how to "trim" his enemies. After I had made several ineffectual attempts to get the fine old fellow away from the one-sided, loquacious interview, he commenced all over again with a long, hard-gripped, affectionate unending see-saw handshake with Sun, declaring:

"Mr. Sen, why can't you have dinner at the hotel with us to-night? It will give us a chance to get better acquainted."

I finally got the good-hearted old chap out of the house, and when I returned Sun confronted me with a comically reproachful look, which led to a hearty laugh, in which I joined, however, quite weakly. This was the last casual visitor I ever took to call on the Reformer.

The happiest memory I have of 29 Rue Molière is not the great dinner which Sun gave me and my wife—undoubtedly the finest dinner I ever ate, carrying a menu of perhaps twoscore dainty dishes, such as the Chinese alone know how to prepare (not common dishes like shark's fins and bird's-nest soup but dove's eggs scalded in oil, fresh almonds with sweet pond-cress, pigeon's eggs stewed with mushrooms, golden pheasant pulped with ham, fresh lily-root salad, and bamboo-shoots as tender as the first sprout of asparagus); but it is the memory of an afternoon visit that I made him in company with my little son who, that day, came with me to Rue Molière dressed up in very new clothes and very enthusiastic with his chance of again visiting the doctor. The doctor received his fervent Chinese salutations for a moment, without response or the flicker of an expression; then he beamed out a smile and look of anticipation, and silently taking little Paul into the dining-room, he stood like a statue, gazing affectionately at the boy, beaming with pleasure at the little lad's repeated shouts of joy. There, on the generous table was a great assortment of just the sort of goodies that the doctor knew Paul would like, which he himself, out of his love for little children, had prepared. Paul lost no time in seating himself before the great board, and the juvenile feast went forward.

"Why do you have so many lovely lichi-nuts?" hinted Paul, wondering at the small mountain of this luscious edible, of which the doctor himself was quite fond, coming as they did from his sunny Kwangtung.

"I have them just for you, Paul," beamed the doctor, and the silent, dignified house-servant himself, now all agleam with smiles, prepared to bundle up the lichi-nuts for Paul. The doctor waved the servant aside and declared that Paul should assist him in properly and safely wrapping up the nuts; and the two made a tender picture—the little child with the golden hair and the muscular, strong tawny figure of Sun—busy with paper and twine, both laughing gleefully as they captured the nuts rolling about the great table; until finally Paul had the precious childhood treasure safely before him, smiling radiantly at the boyish expression on the Reformer's face.

Trivial and frivolous as this incident may appear compared to the more formal endeavor of this volume, I think it is needed to show a quality that is, alas, more lacking among the Chinese than with us; the gentle quality that comes from fatherly fellowship in its attitude toward the child.

Only once has it been my pleasure to meet Sun Yat Sen's son, Tsi Sung Song Fo. The meeting was in San Francisco, during the World's Fair, in 1914, when he gave me and my friends a memorable dinner. He had just been graduated from the University of California (he is also a graduate of Columbia), and I was deeply impressed by his resemblance to his father in many regards. The thought occurred to me when I met Tsi Song Fo that this splendid son, who gives promise of a very great future, got nearer to his father (although most of the time thousands of miles away in exile) than most Chinese lads who were in daily contact with their fathers. And in the love between father and son it seemed to me that I could better understand the success of both.

There will never be a Chinese Napoleon; there will never be a Confucius of the white race. The Napoleonic struggle for individualism was a mere pricked bubble compared to the majestic stream of Confucius's teaching, which, however, reached no Ocean of Learning and touched no Shore of Progress. I think, however, that Confucius (if we can believe his analects) saw in the far perspective of the genius that something was lacking in the great and ancient civilization in which he, those two thousand and more years ago, was still a youth. I think that the great sage saw that just as the Golden Chinese Rule became not negatived but reversed, likewise the cumbrous Chinese ideographs would not allow him to express that sense of duty toward children that in these modern days of occidental progress is the elemental force of our steady advance. Confucius taught filial obedience, but would not China be better off to-day if he had likewise taught more of parental duty?

I have seen Sun Yat Sen in many lights, and my heart has bounded at times at the revelations of the deeper nature of his genius; but I never have felt quite so near to Sun as when he was with children. Verily, not the least among his reform conceptions was that not only should men and women enjoy a perfect liberty in their pilgrimage for better things, but that likewise even the little children should enter into the political and social Kingdom of Heaven.

## XXXIX

### CONCLUSION: SUN THE MORAL FORCE

IN THIS final word of these episodic chapters, I would that I might tell of that full democratic success of the Chinese Republic, for which during the years those of us who have been identified with the Reformer have hoped most ardently. I would that I could tell of a republic in China which, having the sincere support of Japan and of certain other nations of the world, was progressive and prosperous like its happy sister to the west. Alas! different, indeed, are the conditions of these two lands, no longer separated but united by a stretch of water that every day is becoming narrower in its division between the ancient existence of the East and the new life of the West.

At this writing a war is in progress in China between the *tuchun,* supported by the selfish commercial and banking interests of Japan and of certain Christian nations on the one hand, and on the other by Sun Yat Sen, who, with his associates, is still struggling for the democracy of

China. In this struggle, Sun the man of peace has been compelled to become Sun the man of war, for he has put a large army in the field against the enemies of China. Sun's army is strong and well disciplined, but he does not depend upon this army to gain the victory. Beyond this army he possesses a strength far greater than any army can give him. Armies can be defeated, and a victory turned into utter rout, but the power possessed by Sun can never know a defeat and will always go forward in spite of all armed resistance against it; for even the thundering destruction of modern guns cannot destroy its strength. Soldiers are mortal and their guns only good for a certain number of shots; this power will live on forever, and becomes ever stronger with the use to which it is put, for its strength comes from its employment. The bravery of the most intrepid soldier can only come when he takes on this other strength to supplement the weaker strength of his arms.

What is this other strength which supports Sun Yat Sen to-day more than could ever the greatest and proudest army? It is that *moral* strength which, in some measure, great or small, God gives to every man who seeks it sincerely; and to Sun, this moral strength indeed has been given prodigally. Those of us who know Sun intimately look upon him not so much as a man but rather as the moral force which he represents. We see him as in the dissolving view of a calcium-light, showing at one time the man and at the other the spiritual clearness of his moral strength. The humble plowboy of Blue Valley, after years of spiritual development, became the first leverage which, acting from the fulcrum of Chinese town democracies, lifted the sturdy Chinese race out of their ancient lethargy and began to constitute out of the *hsien* a new local autonomy for the eventual political reform of all China.

Why should one lament, however, even after all these years of stern moral effort, that Sun finds himself compelled to organize a great army to defend this democracy from its enemies within and without China? Something of the *lit-she* spirit is ordained to continue a part of this moral force, which above the darkness of the tempest shall gleam out in the very midst of the storm like a lighthouse beating back the waves and showing the charted course to safety beyond.

Sun grows old, but his moral force ever remains young. Sun will pass the way of all mortal men, but this moral force, created by his genius, will live on as long as human history records the better endeavor of man. Hence, were it not for the great suffering which the present *tuchun* war puts upon the patient Chinese masses, it would matter little what the *tuchuns* and their foreign allies do to-day.

For in that morrow of better things, this moral force will be victorious.

# INDEX

369

# INDEX